# GREATER NORTH FULTON
### *Toward the Twenty-First Century*

## TEXT BY KATHY COTE

## PHOTOGRAPHY BY RON SHERMAN

LONGSTREET PRESS
Atlanta, Georgia

PUBLISHED IN COOPERATION WITH
THE GREATER NORTH FULTON CHAMBER OF COMMERCE

Published by LONGSTREET PRESS, INC.,
a subsidiary of Cox Newspapers,
a division of Cox Enterprises, Inc.
2140 Newmarket Parkway, Suite 118
Marietta, Georgia 30067

Printed in the United States of America

1st printing, 1994

ISBN: 1-56352-121-0


This book was printed by Arcata Graphics, Kingsport, Tennessee

Film preparation by Advertising Technologies, Inc., Atlanta, Georgia

Art direction, design, and production by Graham and Company Graphics, Inc., Atlanta, Georgia

# CONTENTS

◆

# FOREWORD

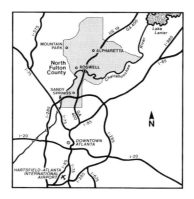

Greater North Fulton County's beauty, style and progressive attitude have made it one of the fastest-growing areas in the country, yet it remains uncrowded, relaxed and peaceful. North Fulton County is committed to the achievement of both business and personal goals and the relentless pursuit of quality that has attracted more than 150,000 people in the past 15 years.

Included in the North Fulton County area are Sandy Springs, Roswell, Alpharetta, Mountain Park, and unincorporated Fulton County, north of the Atlanta city limits. Together, they offer a unique history, welcoming attitude, strong community spirit, and responsive local government.

In the midst of expansive growth, local city and county governments, business leaders and residents have worked together to insure that the area's high quality of life remains intact. As a result, North Fulton County has an award-winning educational system, nationally acclaimed parks and recreation departments, numerous progressive and growing churches, diverse health-care facilities and services, and an extremely low crime rate. The growth of the Georgia 400 "Golden Corridor" has also lured corporations such as American Honda, AT&T, Digital Equipment Corporation, Ciba Vision, Herman Miller, Kimberly-Clark, Siemens, State Farm, Southern Bell, and UPS to establish operations in North Fulton County. These major employers and a growing small business community, combined with the support of state and local governments, maintain a thriving retail and business community.

The Greater North Fulton area was recently named one of the most rapidly developing/expanding and most outstanding places in the metro Atlanta area to live and work. Our communities rank 1, 2, & 3 in a quality of life study by Atlanta magazine. With its serene beauty and high quality of life, North Fulton will continue to be the most desirable address in the metro area as it moves toward the twenty-first century.

*John M. Dorris*
*President and CEO*
*Greater North Fulton Chamber of Commerce*

# INTRODUCTION

◆

North Fulton County is a beautiful suburban enclave of the thriving city of Atlanta, the hub of the South and one of the largest metropolitan areas in the nation.

Characterized for generations by softly rolling green hills of open farmland and charming small towns, the collection of communities north of Atlanta has embraced the challenges of the next century by welcoming growth and developing an outstanding blend of the finest living, working and recreational environments.

North Fulton County epitomizes the forward-thinking character of the New South in communities which respect the value of the historic past while creating a vision for the future. Generations have helped the area to become a culturally rich, racially diverse, economically sound community where the unique charm of rural life in an historically significant environment is subtly united with the cultural and economic assets of an urban lifestyle.

Residents of North Fulton take pride in their environment, their schools, their neighborhoods, their churches, their government and their business leaders.

Today, the ancestral homes built by the early settlers along the banks of the Chattahoochee River in the "enchanted land" of North Fulton are part of a cherished legacy, meticulously preserved for future generations. The changing skyline and brightly lit geometric frames topping the twin towers at the perimeter are part of the vision for North Fulton's future.

Responsive local governments are attracting a business environment that is supportive of community organizations and provides employment opportunities and sound economic footing for future growth. The area has been described as a major employment center in its own right by the Atlanta Regional Commission, with more than 34,000 North Fulton-based jobs at the beginning of the 1990s.

As economic development continues to tunnel up the "Golden Corridor" of Georgia 400, the main artery through North Fulton, voices in the business community are anxious to jump on the bandwagon of success. Studies have shown that North Fulton will get 80 percent of the growth in Fulton County well into the next century.

The population influx in recent years has made the young, vibrant community of North Fulton a residential hub characterized by prosperous neighborhoods and luxurious country club developments built around championship golf courses. The low median age of North Fulton residents and high per-capita median income insure a high quality of family life, a dedication to the finest recreational amenities and a communitywide commitment to safety and prosperity.

# THE HISTORIC ROOTS OF NORTH FULTON COUNTY

◆

North Fulton County is an area rich in history and committed to its past. The early settlers were true pioneers, establishing sprawling farms and thriving towns in the vast countryside once occupied by Creek and Cherokee Indians along the Chattahoochee River.

The area now known as Sandy Springs was named for the bubbling waters discovered in a sand pit near present-day Mt. Vernon Highway in the early 1800s. The land was inhabited by Creek Indians until the land cession of 1821, and the springs were an important landmark, sitting at the crossroads of two Indian trails.

In the original distribution of five counties, Sandy Springs was part of District 17, Henry County, and later became part of the land package that created DeKalb County. Land was then distributed by lottery to residents of the county.

While the first settlers were establishing farms and homesteads in the rolling hills of Sandy Springs, the first gold rush had begun in the nearby North Georgia mountains. When Benjamin Parks discovered gold in Dahlonega in 1828, prospectors rushed to the rich waters of Georgia's Chattahoochee, Chestatee and Etowah rivers in hopes of finding their fortunes.

A year later, Roswell King, a coastal planter and manager of the vast Butler Plantation in Darien, Georgia, was sent by the Bank of Darien to investi-

gate the possibility of establishing a branch of the bank in the gold-rush town of Auraria.

The 64-year-old coastal farmer was entranced by the cooler climate, the lush timberland and the potential of the rushing waters of the rivers in the Cherokee Indian territory known as "the enchanted land" because it bordered the Chattahoochee River.

In 1837, while Cherokee Indians still occupied the land, King returned and through the government land lottery, laid claim to property overlooking the Chattahoochee River near the roaring waters of Vickery Creek.

The following year more than 13,000 Indians in Georgia and Alabama were moved westward by the U.S. Army in the infamous "Trail of Tears."

Early settlers of present-day North Fulton often traded at the Dorris Store, near Crabapple, or the Howell Brothers General Store at Lebanon on Vickery Creek. Families like the Ruckers and Hembrees, who lived in log cabins in what is now Alpharetta, farmed the sprawling land and traded freely with the local Indians.

According to local historians, later generations of the Rucker clan established the Rucker Cotton Seed Company and one of the area's earliest newspapers, the *Alpharetta Free Press*. Members of the Hembree clan organized the Lebanon Baptist Church in 1836 in Roswell.

With the help of his two sons and slaves brought

from the coastal plantation, Roswell King was able to begin construction almost immediately on a dam and millrace on Vickery Creek to supply power for

*Roswell Mill*

the Roswell Cotton Mills, which took three years to complete. The long, narrow mill building was built right below the dam and connected to a machine shop and nearby blacksmith shop.

The state of Georgia was petitioned for incorporation of the mills in 1839 and provisions were made at that time for additional cotton or woolen mills, sawmills and grist mills to be added at the discretion of the stockholders.

The land surrounding Roswell King's modest log cabin, affectionately known as "the castle," was now safe for settlement and he invited his family and friends from coastal Georgia to join him in this new territory. Settlers quickly came and the town sprang up with the trappings of a traditional New England village, reflecting King's Connecticut roots.

Most of the early settlers, who named the town Roswell after founding father Roswell King, were farmers, blacksmiths, rock masons, carpenters, merchants, mill hands and explorers.

Most of Roswell's early residents were of the Baptist or Methodist faith and the first organized church, founded in 1836, was known as the Mount Carmel Methodist Church. It later became the Roswell United Methodist Church, which is one of the area's largest churches today.

The founding father brought slaves from Darien to help build settlers' homes and engaged a New England architect, Willis Ball, to design the early structures. The Minhinnett brothers of Plymouth, England, a stonemason and craftsman, were hired to oversee construction. Roswell's first permanent dwelling, Primrose Cottage, was built for Roswell King's widowed daughter, Eliza King Hand, in 1839.

Primrose Cottage was built for an urban lifestyle, differing significantly from the rural homes of that period. The four-on-four construction allows the rooms to flow easily for a gracious style of living. The New England-style home still has the original flooring, seven fireplaces and the historically significant hand-turned rosemary pine fence which lines the walk along Mimosa Boulevard. Visitors to the Roswell landmark enjoy the grounds with the secluded rear gardens (designed around one of Georgia's oldest live oak trees), original summer kitchen, wine cellar and terraced garden with brick patio. The property was purchased for use as a special events facility by Magic Moments, a Norcross-based catering firm, in 1991. Minor adjustments have been made to the elegant interior, including construction of a 1,200-square-foot ballroom in the rear.

The Roswell Presbyterian Church was organized by a group of settlers in the parlor of Primrose Cottage in 1839. Dr. Nathaniel Alpheus Pratt, pastor of the Darien Presbyterian Church, was invited to come and lead the congregation.

Construction began immediately on the Doric-columned, white clapboard Presbyterian church on Mimosa Boulevard, located on land donated by Roswell King. The towering, fluted columns and wide pedimented portico reflect the influence of the designer, Willis Ball.

When the church was completed in 1840, settlers turned out each week to sit in the box pews and listen to sermons from the high center pulpit. A special gallery overlooking the congregation was used by the slaves from neighboring homes.

The Independent Presbyterian Church in Savannah presented the fledgling congregation with a ship's bell, cast in bronze in Philadelphia in 1827, for the squat bell tower of the church. The resounding tones of that gift are still heard on Roswell's historic square today.

A two-room schoolhouse, the Academy, was built on land donated by Roswell King adjacent to the Presbyterian church. The Reverend A. H. Hand was invited to come from Augusta as the first schoolteacher to the children of Roswell's founding families. Although the building was not preserved, the site of the Academy has been used in an educational capacity until present day.

Several other properties were completed in Roswell between 1840 and 1842, specifically the Bricks, Bulloch Hall, Barrington Hall, Mimosa Hall and Great Oaks. Many of these stately homes are still private residences, preserved by generations committed to their inestimable historical value. Others have been restored and are used as light commercial property.

The mill workers' housing constructed in the early 1840s consisted of townhome-style apartments surrounded by small New England "saltbox" cottages. Today, the two masonry buildings known as the Bricks have been fully restored for use as a private dining facility. The wide, hand-planed floorboards held down by square nails and the large fireplace mantels dating from the original construction create a unique ambience in the modest buildings overlooking the Roswell Mill. Many of the quaint cottages in the village are still standing, occupied by descendants of the original mill workers.

One of the most significant construction projects in the early years of the village was the home of Roswell King's son Barrington, who moved to the area to help his father establish the mill. Barrington King, his wife Catherine Nephew King and their eight children lived in Barrington Hall, a classic Greek revival home which anchors one end of Roswell Square. The home, surrounded on three sides by stately white columns in the pure Temple style, was designed by Connecticut architect Willis Ball. Today, it is still owned and occupied by a direct descendant of Barrington King.

Willis Ball is also credited with the columned facade of neighboring Bulloch Hall, now a multi-use facility owned by the city of Roswell. Originally built for James Bulloch, president of the Savannah

*Magnolia Ball*

branch of the Bank of the United States, the full pedimented portico and four Doric columns on the front piazza made an ideal setting for the Christmas wedding of Mittie Bulloch to Theodore Roosevelt in 1853.

Bulloch Hall, which sat vacant for twenty years, was restored to its original grandeur by local developer Richard Myrick, who purchased the property in 1971. In 1978, the city purchased it for use as the focal point of Roswell's Historic District.

Bulloch Hall sits in historic splendor at the top of Bulloch Avenue, flanked by Mimosa Hall and Dolvin House, two private residences that date from the late 1800s. On the south side, Emily Dolvin, aunt of former President Jimmy Carter, lives in the saltbox-style house built by J. M. Penland, a local storeowner. Mrs. Dolvin was instrumental in the organization of the Roswell Historical Society and the ensuing preservation of area homes.

*Historic Glenridge Hall*

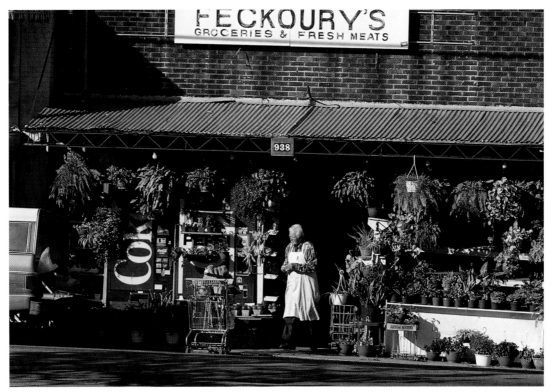

*Feckoury's Store*

Off the north wing of Bulloch Hall, Mimosa Hall was built by John Dunwoody, a coastal planter who settled in the Roswell area. The original structure burned during the housewarming party and was renamed Phoenix Hall, after being rebuilt with stucco scored to look like brick. In 1867, the house became the property of Andrew Jackson Hansell, president of the Roswell Manufacturing Company, and has since been occupied by six generations of the Hansell family.

For a brief period, the home was owned by renowned architect Neel Reid, who designed the gardens and laid a stone courtyard in the shape of a champagne glass.

Further down Mimosa Boulevard, Holly Hill, a raised Greek revival-style cottage, was built by Roswell King in 1845 as a summer home for Savannah cotton broker Robert Lewis. The columned front and rear porches of the charming exterior were restored by Mr. and Mrs. Robert Sommerville and the home is still used as a private residence today.

Great Oaks, a Georgian Colonial home on Mimosa Boulevard, has also been maintained by direct descendants of Roswell's founding fathers. The home was built in 1842 for Roswell King's daughter and her husband, Reverend Nathaniel Pratt, who led the newly formed Presbyterian church. Local clay was used to construct the 18-inch-thick brick walls laid in Flemish bond.

Several other pre–Civil War buildings have been preserved in the Upper Roswell Square near the Canton Street shopping district and Heart of Roswell Park.

Naylor Hall, on Canton Street, was built by Barrington King in 1840 as a private home for the Roswell Mill manager Hugh Proudfoot. During the Civil War all but four rooms were destroyed. Subsequent additions have restored the columned entrance and side portico to their original splendor.

In the 1930s the property was sold to Colonel Harrison Broadwell, who made some structural modifications and named it Naylor Hall. The columns, portico and handmade wood trimwork were added to enhance the original facade. Since 1987, with the addition of a ballroom capable of seating 150 people, it has functioned as a special events facility.

The Roswell Mill complex doubled in size during the 1850s, and the Ivy Woolen Mills were added at that time. On Vickery Creek just below the existing cotton mill, the Roswell Manufacturing Company was a thriving industry, employing approximately 150 people.

South of the Chattahoochee River, the large rural community of Sandy Springs was also beginning to develop, with churches and modest farmhouses being built by early settlers. The springs for which the area is named were an important landmark to the founders of the community, who established the first Methodist church under a brush arbor at the site in 1848. A permanent preacher could not be found so the young congregation was led by different preachers passing through on their way to Atlanta.

Several years later, five acres of the property surrounding the springs was donated by Willson Spruill, one of the early settlers, and a one-room log building was constructed to serve as a schoolroom and a place of worship. In 1866 a frame building replaced the log structure of the Sandy Springs United Methodist Church and was used until 1920 when a brick structure was erected.

It wasn't until 1853 that Sandy Springs became part of Fulton County, when the county was formed out of portions of Cherokee, Coweta, Fayette, Henry and Gwinnett counties to establish a county for the growing city of Atlanta. Historians suggest that Fulton County acquired its name from either Robert Fulton, inventor of the steam engine, or Hamilton Fulton, the first chief engineer of the state of Georgia.

The first school in Sandy Springs was built in 1851 directly across from the church property. When the building burned in 1897, local citizens with the help of the Fulton County Board of Education built a four-room, two-story school which was named the Hammond School after a prominent Fulton County lawyer and educator.

When Fulton County was established, it was governed by a panel of five justices, known as the Inferior Court. In 1880, this governing body was replaced with a separate five-member Board of Commissioners for Roads and Revenues. Board members were selected by the Grand Jury and served a three-year term. A decade later the law was changed to allow qualified voters to select the board members.

While Fulton County quickly became the largest urban area in the south, few adjustments were made to its style of governing. Not until 1968 was the board's name changed to the Fulton County Board of Commissioners and, within a few years, expanded to seven members.

Today, three at-large and four district commissioners are each elected to four-year terms. The chairman is elected by the voters and then a vice chairman is selected by the board.

Sandy Springs was linked to its northern neighbors by a covered bridge built in 1856 across the Chattahoochee River. Although damaged heavily during the Civil War, the bridge was rebuilt by the Confederate Army and used until 1925. It was

*Magnolia Ball*

11

*Christmas at Bulloch Hall*

eventually replaced by a two-lane concrete bridge capable of handling the increased automobile traffic at that time.

Residents of Sandy Springs could make the journey to the foot of the river on a one-car railroad train, the Roswell Railroad, which ran twice daily from 1880 to 1924. Its sole engineer, Ike Roberts, made the trek each day from Roswell Junction (present-day Chamblee) to a depot on the southeastern banks of the Chattahoochee River.

The Chattahoochee River has always played a critical role in the community of North Fulton. In 1904 the river was dammed at Morgan Falls to provide the first electricity to the area.

During the Civil War, most of the stately mansions in Roswell served as hospitals, barracks and command headquarters for the Union army during the occupation of the town, thus sparing them from a blazing demise like the rest of Atlanta. The Bricks, identified by historians as some of the oldest apartments in the United States, escaped the fiery path of destruction by functioning as a hospital for wounded soldiers. Historians believe that Union officers were headquartered at Barrington Hall and Great Oaks and that Bulloch Hall was used as a barracks while Federal troops planned the Battle of Atlanta.

The Roswell Mills were one of the primary manufacturing facilities for the famous "Confederate Gray" uniforms. When Union troops took over the city on July 16, 1864, the mills were burned and more than 400 women and children who had been working at the site were charged with treason and sent north for imprisonment. After the war, many returned to re-establish roots in the Roswell area.

The mills of the Roswell Manufacturing Company were rebuilt during the reconstruction period but a fire in 1926 completely destroyed the cotton mill. The Ivy Woolen Mill was incorporated in 1873 as Laurel Mills and the only other business, the Lebanon Flour Mill, eventually liquidated.

The new mill constructed by the Roswell Manufacturing Company in 1882 was purchased by Southern Mills, Inc. in 1948 and remained in operation until 1975. The remains of the cotton mill are being excavated by archaeologists and identified by historians today, while the former Southern Mills

facility has been converted into an entertainment complex currently in use in historic Roswell.

Artifacts recovered from the original mill site are being collected for use in a Water Power Museum currently being developed in Roswell. Under the direction of the Georgia Office of Historic Preservation, North Fulton historians and interested business owners are researching the industrial background of

*Williams/Payne House*

the area and compiling information about the vital role of water in the textile mills that operated along Vickery Creek for the last two centuries.

Exhibits will simulate the actual operation of the textile mills from the 1830s to the 1970s and include machinery and equipment from past excavation efforts of the original mill site and donations by county residents. Developers will work from the original design specifications of the mill which were done by a firm from Patterson, New Jersey and date from 1839.

Like many North Fulton preservation projects, the Water Power Museum has received remarkable support from the community. In addition to vital information and funding, irreplaceable items like an original spindle and dray tickets dating back to 1882 have been donated by city residents.

Although many of the historic properties in North Fulton have undergone physical changes over the years, one landmark remains untouched by the passage of time, a testimony to life in rural Georgia in the pre–Civil War period.

The Smith Plantation, an eight-room farmhouse built in 1844 near the Upper Roswell Square to insure privacy and tranquility for the very religious Smith family, is an undisturbed testament to rural life in the 19th century. The 300-acre estate once used for farming and cotton still has the original well, antique corncrib and servants quarters.

After the Civil War, Archibald Smith's daughter Lizzie lived in the house until her death in 1915. The house was closed until Archibald Jr., grandson of the original builder, and his wife Mary began renovations in 1940. They converted the traditional single-story farmhouse porch to a two-story facade with columns, and added gas street-lamps imported from England.

When Mrs. Smith died in 1981 the property was inherited by her niece, Mrs. James L. Skinner of Decatur. Although no members of the Skinner family have ever lived in the house, they are committed to its historic significance.

The contents of the home, which were cataloged and photographed by Dr. James Lester Skinner III, an English professor at Presbyterian College in South Carolina, have been left intact for public viewing with the exception of some documents that were turned over to the state archives and some artifacts which were donated to the Atlanta Historical Society.

The Smith Plantation has been described by many as a secret "time capsule" bursting with historic treasures from diaries to farming tools, and one of the best examples of mid-19th-century farming life in North Fulton.

The majority of the Plantation acreage on Alpharetta Highway was sold to the city of Roswell in 1986 for development of the Municipal Complex, public library, auditorium and park space. The Roswell Historical Society conducts tours of the Smith Plantation. In addition to the main farmhouse, visitors are encouraged to tour the original outbuildings on the property including the kitchen, corncrib, servants quarters and barn.

*Exterior Bullock Hall, Christmas*

# THE CITIES AND COMMUNITIES OF NORTH FULTON

◆

Northern Fulton County includes the incorporated cities of Roswell, Alpharetta and Mountain Park, as well as the vast unincorporated areas of Sandy Springs, Crabapple and Shakerag.

While many of the characteristics that create the quality of life associated with North Fulton are uniform throughout the area, each community has specific traits that make it uniquely different from its neighbors.

The fast-paced shopping mecca along Roswell Road in Sandy Springs, the sprawling horse farms in Crabapple, the rolling golf courses in Alpharetta and the charm of the historic homes in Roswell create a special ambiance in each community that is reflected in the businesses, civic organizations and 150,000 residents that call North Fulton home.

The elected officials, police departments, fire and emergency services, medical facilities, schools, parks and libraries, which vary by area, also reflect the size, growth and stability of each piece of the North Fulton pie.

Sandy Springs, the largest unincorporated area in the United States, represents a significant portion of that pie. The 23,748 acres of the community are bounded by the Chattahoochee River to the north and west, Atlanta on the south and DeKalb and Gwinnett Counties on the east.

Creek Indians settled the area in the 1500s, attracted by the springs which were located at the intersection of two major Indian trails, present-day Roswell Road and Mount Vernon Highway.

During the reapportionment of land following the resettlement of the Indian tribes in the early 1800s, farmland in Sandy Springs was distributed to settlers by lottery. The new community of farmers were soon building homes, churches and small stores in the rich countryside.

Sandy Springs was the first community to become part of Fulton County. It was absorbed into Fulton in 1853, when portions of Cherokee, Coweta, Fayette, Henry and Gwinnett counties were used to establish a county for the growing city of Atlanta.

For almost a century, Sandy Springs remained a farming community, a small crossroads town between the rural farms of the countryside and the urban setting of Atlanta. It was not until the growth from the city of Atlanta began to move north in the early 1950s, that residential and commercial development began at a rapid pace. At that time, Sandy Springs became a popular bedroom community for Atlanta and the population skyrocketed.

As an unincorporated area, growth in Sandy Springs continued virtually unchecked for decades. Futile attempts to regulate development were made by groups like the Community Planning Council, a group of local residents and county representatives who met in 1968 to draw up a comprehensive

*Old Soldiers Day, Alpharetta*

development plan for the area, but most efforts were quickly abandoned and essentially ineffective.

The 1980s brought a fresh wave of interest in beautification and revitalization of the commercial district of Sandy Springs. From this grew the Sandy Springs Historic Community Foundation, a volunteer group of residents who have made great strides in community involvement with the creation of an historic site and annual festival.

Today, Sandy Springs is considered one of Atlanta's most prestigious suburbs. Luxurious suburban developments, the finest public and private schools, excellent recreational amenities and close proximity to the heart of Atlanta make it an attractive residential and commercial location.

A vibrant revitalization effort is again attracting attention to the thriving community. For the last several years a grassroots movement has taken shape to refurbish the commercial strip along Roswell Road north of the perimeter and restrict additional development. Residents are tackling civic issues, water usage, park space and visual pollution through signage, head on.

Progress has been slow but positive results are forthcoming. Community groups like Sandy Springs/ North Fulton Clean & Beautiful, the Historic Community Foundation, the Greater North Fulton Chamber of Commerce, and arts groups based in Sandy Springs are working closely with various arms of the Fulton County government to address community concerns and plan for the future.

Armed with innovative long-range goals, a strong base of more than 80,000 residents, and with as much upscale commercial office space along the perimeter as in downtown Atlanta, Sandy Springs is a drawing card for North Fulton.

As essential as revitalization is to Sandy Springs, preservation is to residents in other pockets of unincorporated North Fulton. The tiny district of Shakerag—a one-stop-sign area of unincorporated Fulton County off Georgia Highway 141 at McGinniss Ferry Road—maintains its roots as a sparsely populated rural community.

This section of North Fulton, only three miles wide, sits on the border of Fulton, Forsyth and Gwinnett Counties, and at one time served as the seat of government for Old Milton County. Early settlers reached the area via a ferry system established by a man named McGinniss shortly after Gwinnett County was formed in 1818. According to annals compiled by local historians, the ferry traveled down the Chattahoochee River from a site two miles west of Suwanee to a settlement called Sheltonville. Years later, gold was found in the area and Sheltonville became a thriving business community. Evidence of surface mining done near Shakerag at Cauley Creek and Cowpen Branch can still be identified today.

According to local folklore, two miners got into a fight and began tearing at each other's clothes, hence the name "Shakerag" was born. Many of the roads are named after these mining families who settled in the area to farm and raise livestock. One home, a favorite for visitors to the quaint farming village, was ordered from the Sears & Roebuck catalog of 1907. The 1,800-square-foot pre-fabricated home, which is owned by the Strickland family, was shipped by rail and then sent across the river by ferry before being assembled at its current location.

From street names to social functions, the Shakerag community is committed to tradition. The Shady Grove Baptist Church, established in 1838, still sits in the heart of the area, and a hunt club formed by local residents in 1941 is still actively supported by local families.

When growth spread into the northern reaches of

*Mountain Park Lake*

# Zachary Henderson

When the city of Roswell decided to break a century of tradition and add new buildings in the historic town square, the logical choice for planning and design was local architect Zachary Henderson.

When the owners of the only contemporary building in Roswell's Canton Street Historic District decided it was time to look a bit more like their neighbors, they also called Mr. Henderson to perform the magical transformation.

And when the Alpharetta Historical Society was given the historic Mansell House as their new home with the stipulation that they move it across North Fulton, they too went knocking on Zach Henderson's door for help.

A familiar name and face since the boom years began in North Fulton, Mr. Henderson has made historic architecture his area of expertise and put a distinctive stamp of traditional, quality design on countless county landmarks.

A third-generation horseman, Mr. Henderson started his own firm in the rural North Fulton countryside in 1965 and immediately became active in community concerns regarding growth and controlled development.

He was instrumental in forming the North Fulton Chamber of Commerce in the early 1970s and more recently was in the charter group that established the Historic Roswell District Owners and Business Association.

Mr. Henderson's Roswell architectural firm has helped to shape the face of the 640-acre Roswell Historic District that stretches from the Chattahoochee River to Woodstock Road by participating in fifteen different design projects.

In the late 1970s a preservation society was formed by the merchants on Canton Street to recycle some of the older homes for commercial use. Now a quaint strip of antique shops and cozy professional offices, Canton Street is a thriving business district with the unusual charm and appeal of a small town's main street.

The "Shops on the Square" in Roswell are further evidence of Mr. Henderson's commitment to preserving the area's historic atmosphere. Designed as a large two-story building with retail shops on the ground floor and office space upstairs, the corner project has box fronts which create the illusion of unique, individual store fronts for each shop. Since completion in 1985, the project has been so successful that retail stores now occupy both floors. Like much of the architect's work, the little shops fit so well with existing historic structures that they are often mistaken for original buildings.

This blending of the old and new is also evident in other renovation projects by Mr. Henderson around North Fulton including the Mansell House, the banquet addition to the antebellum Naylor Hall, the education building and gym at the Howard School's north campus near the Chattahoochee River and even the architect's private home on an 11-acre farm off Birmingham Highway in Crabapple.

Fulton County and the sleepy setting began to attract developers, local residents formed the Shakerag Civic Association to keep a check on commercial and residential construction. The group, formed in 1988 as a social organization, was instrumental in facilitating the purchase of 165 acres of Chattahoochee River frontage by the National Park Service for use as a natural wildlife preserve. The Association works closely with key players at John's Creek, a mixed-use development owned by Technology Park adjacent to Shakerag.

Another charming spot in unincorporated North Fulton is Crabapple, a quiet crossroads where horse farms and antique shops have created a quaint residential haven five miles north of Roswell, at a suburban five-points, the corner of Birmingham Highway and Mayfield, Broadwell, Mid-Broadwell and Crabapple roads.

According to local historians the area was not settled until after the Civil War, when farmers came to the area to raise cotton. It is believed that the community got its name in 1874 when the first school was built in a grove of crabapple trees. It was also recognized in farming circles for an unusual strain of "double-jointed" cotton which was native to Crabapple and raised by John Broadwell in the early 1900s.

In the early 1960s Emory and Virginia Reeves moved their prosperous antique business from the bustle of East Paces Ferry in Buckhead to a quiet, remote site called Crabapple Corners. Over a vintage bottle of ice-cold Coke, Mr. Reeves, the unofficial mayor of the one-stop community, can still recall the unique charm that was a natural characteristic of Crabapple prior to the sudden growth and surge of residential development in the area.

His store, Crabapple Corners, is housed in the century-old general mercantile building and offers country-style gifts, collectibles and home accessories. Each May, thousands of Atlanta shoppers gather at the tiny storefront to enjoy the Crabapple

*Roswell church raising*

21

*Pat Williams, spring plowing*

Antique Festival, a community tradition for more than twenty years.

Historic preservation is a priority for both old-timers and newcomers to the charming village of Crabapple. In the 1970s, Ruby and Lloyd Pittman developed the area's original cotton gin into the Raven's Nest, a spacious, formal setting for paintings and antiques. During the holiday season, Ms. Pittman offers her customers goodies baked in an antique, hand-painted Dutch warming stove.

In addition to preserving the cotton gin, the Pittmans were behind the effort to save the original home of another one of Alpharetta's earliest families. They purchased, moved and renovated the John B. Broadwell House, which dates from the early 1800s and now serves as a charming restaurant adjacent to the furniture gallery.

The Pittmans purchased the historic home for the amazing sum of $1 from owner Lamar Tucker and moved the 130-year-old building a precarious journey of three blocks along Mayfield Road. During the 18-month restoration, the home was stripped down to the original heart-pine walls and gradually refurbished. Once completed, the rustic ambiance and period furnishings became a beautiful complement to the home-cooked flavors and traditional menu offered at Mr. John B.'s, a popular location for dining out in North Fulton.

Just as the unincorporated areas of North Fulton vary in size and style, so too do the three incorporated cities of Mountain Park, Roswell and Alpharetta.

North Fulton's smallest city, indeed one of the smallest cities in the state, is Mountain Park, a rustic residential community surrounding two lakes on the border of Cherokee and Fulton counties.

The area was settled in the 1920s as a popular summer mountain retreat for Atlanta families hoping to escape the unrelenting heat of the city. Wealthy homeowners built unusual, rustic country cottages, many of which are still in use by the environmentalists, artists and musicians that have gravitated to the area since the turn of the century.

Mountain Park, designated an environmental refuge by the state, is a sanctuary for animals such as deer, bobcat and muskrats, and birds like the blue heron, red-tailed hawk, and eastern bluebird. As a tribute to its naturalist setting, the streets on the north side of Lake Garrett and Lake Cherful are named after trees, and roads on the south side are named after birds.

The city was incorporated in 1927 and is currently governed by a mayor and seven council members elected by the 600 city residents. Peter Packard serves as mayor of Mountain Park until 1995. Until the 1930s, water for Mountain Park homes was acquired from a natural spring, but that was eventually closed and water is now purchased from the

Cobb and Fulton County systems. A volunteer fire department and small police department provide protection and emergency services for Mountain Park citizens. The city also operates a swimming pool and civic center which is used for meetings of community organizations and special events like the annual chili cook-off.

Although considerably larger, the neighboring community of Alpharetta has maintained the small-town charm of a city with rural roots. Founded and incorporated in 1858, Alpharetta was a trading post on the Cherokee Indian trail between the mountains of North Georgia and the banks of the Chattahoochee River. The town was originally called New Prospect Campground and then became Alpharetta, which is Greek for "first town."

Alpharetta was a thriving cotton community and the county seat of Old Milton County through the turn of the century. During the Depression, when the price of cotton dropped from $10 a bale to $1, the fragile economic structure of the rural area collapsed. At that time, Roswell was part of Cobb County, but the city was released to join Alpharetta and become part of Fulton County.

After Fulton County adopted Milton County in 1932, all of the major roads were paved, and water, drainage and sewer systems were installed. For generations, Alpharetta remained a cotton and farming community until the building boom of the last twenty years spread north and began to develop in pockets around the city's twenty square miles.

During the 1950s and '60s Alpharetta became a popular residential area for employees of AT&T, Siemens, Kimberly-Clark, UPS, and other large corporations in downtown Atlanta. In the 1970s the horseback-riding industry boomed and development of large tracts of land into residential sites and golf courses began.

Since then, growth in Alpharetta has never wavered. The city's population has leaped from a mere 3,000 people in 1980 to more than 19,600 today. Population projections based on current trends indicate the potential for 85,000 residents by the year 2010, with an employment population of over 200,000.

Today Alpharetta is a thriving hub for luxurious residential communities and sprawling commercial developments, attracting an impressive corporate business roster with names like AT&T, Digital, Mobil Land Development (GA) Corp., Siemens, Honda and Equifax.

*House Representative Dorothy Felton*

Mayor Jimmy Phillips, a city administrator and six city councilmen are divided into committees to oversee city finance, courts, human resources, police and fire, planning and inspections, solid waste and water. Together, they work to preserve a high standard of living through careful facilities management.

In keeping with the city's motto, "Progress in Progress," local officials are currently working on a downtown development plan to boost retail use of the central business district and develop a theme for the Main Street community of retailers.

Several businesses on Alpharetta's Main Street epitomize the small-town charm that provides such a unique slice of Southern life. Since 1920, local folks have gathered at Alpha Soda to savor the latest gossip and feast on home-cooked Southern staples. Although the location has changed over the years, the atmosphere has never varied.

Another institution on Alpharetta's Main Street is the Alpharetta Bargain Store, which features a smorgasbord of merchandise accumulated from stores going out of business, manufacturers' overruns and retail end lots haphazardly displayed in a sprawling 20,000-square-foot building.

The business was initially established by local entrepreneur Buck Burgess, who sold dresses off the back of his pickup truck to North Fulton housewives

*Martin's Landing Lake*

in the 1950s. The growth of the Bargain Store's reputation for high-quality designer labels at bargain-basement prices has grown almost as rapidly as the city of Alpharetta and now it is not unusual to see some of Atlanta's most affluent shoppers at the store, prowling through thousands of women's shoes and sportswear items.

Small-town stores also work their magic on the visitors and residents of nearby Roswell, the largest city in North Fulton. A virtual institution on the historic stretch of Canton Street is "Papa Fred's Store," where owner Fred Funderbunk tended flowers from the back of his pickup truck and held court with visitors to the quaint shopping district for decades. Originally a dry goods store opened by Michael Feckoury in 1908, the market now provides color and charm to all of the storefronts with an abundance of colorful hanging flower baskets. Inside, an interesting jumble of food staples, canning supplies and antique farm equipment can be found, still for sale.

Next door, the old Roswell movie theater has

*Old Soldiers Day, Alpharetta*

been converted into several antique shops and a small restaurant. Mittie's Tea Room, named after famous Roswell resident Martha Bulloch Roosevelt, is in a tiny nook in the former projection room upstairs and serves a mixture of delectable sandwiches, salads and sweets.

Professionals with offices on Canton Street, like local architect Zachary Henderson and U.S. Representative Tom Campbell, often amble along the shaded street for a quiet bite of lunch in the quaint restaurants near the town square.

Another popular stop along Canton Street is the Moss Blacksmith Shop where Roswell's former fire chief Ken Moss does custom ironwork design, restoration and repairs in a garage behind the old Methodist parsonage. In keeping with his family tradition, Mr. Moss learned the blacksmithing business as a child, working in the family shop in Buckhead, and opened his own business after settling in Roswell decades ago.

All of these businesses reflect the commitment to tradition and family values that put Roswell in the national spotlight as one of the top fifty places to live in the United States. The popular North Fulton community was featured in a segment by daytime talk-show host Oprah Winfrey, which focused on the area's affordable cost of living, low crime rate, clean environment and superior schools.

The city is also featured as the only Georgia municipality in the book *Fifty Fabulous Places To Raise Your Family*. North Fulton's largest city earned strong points from authors Lee and Saralee Rosenberg, who evaluated communities all across the country. Roswell was praised as having a "hometown" feel, a visionary city government, a strong regional economy, great neighborhoods and schools, an outstanding parks program and excellent transportation.

The success of Roswell today is firmly rooted in the vision and dedication of the area's earliest settlers, especially founder Roswell King. As one of Georgia's first planned communities, Roswell was developed in the 1830s to resemble a New England town built around a square. The firm economic base of the mill industry, the picturesque location on the banks of the Chattahoochee River and the

*Parade, Sandy Springs*

abundance of rich farmland in Roswell became the critical ingredients in a progressive plan for the future.

For more than a century, the thriving mill town was home to a small group of residents, equally divided between rural farm owners and urban workers at the mill. It was not until Roswell was absorbed into Fulton County in 1932 that the door was opened for the unprecedented growth that has made it the sixth-largest city in the state.

According to current national census figures, Roswell is one of the fastest-growing small towns in the United States. Statistics show that as far into the 20th century as 1970, the population of Roswell was still only 5,430. Two decades later, according to the U.S. census digests, it is 49,087 with an estimated growth to 72,000 by the turn of the century.

Part of Roswell's growth is attributed to aggressive annexation begun by Mayor Charles Abercrombie in 1962 and perpetuated by Mayor Pug Mabry, who has led the city through the "boom" years. In the last decade, as different parts of the community have expressed a desire for city services and a voice in city government, more than 4,500 acres of surrounding North Fulton have been annexed into the Roswell city limits.

Currently, 80 percent of Roswell is residential and the remaining 20 percent is mixed office, government and commercial development.

Since its founding as a mill town, the commercial development in Roswell has always been carefully controlled by city government. The 11-member Roswell Historic Preservation Commission, created by the city in 1987, oversees all zoning and signage requests in the 640 acres designated as the city historic district.

The group meets regularly and has been a vital link in preserving the stately grace of the community while welcoming new commercial ventures. Mayor Mabry, who instituted the first planning commission and zoning regulations, is credited with attracting to the area light industry like Herman Miller and Kimberly-Clark, two large employers who adapt well to the characteristics of the community.

In addition to the mayor, Roswell's city government consists of an appointed city administrator and a six-person elected city council. The governing body oversees six targeted areas of city government, specifically: public works, recreation and parks/fire and safety, administration, finance/personnel, environmental concerns and public safety.

Effective city government, high-quality schools, topnotch recreational amenities, an affordable cost of living and the irreplaceable value of historically significant properties make Roswell—and all of North Fulton—one of the most desirable places to live in suburban Atlanta.

# THE INFRASTRUCTURE OF NORTH FULTON COUNTY

◆

P ublic services in the three incorporated cities of North Fulton work hard to keep pace with the demands of a dynamic, growing community. Curbside recycling, state-of-the-art emergency services and outstanding fire protection are standard in each area, facilitated by the highest-quality equipment.

On a county level, water, transportation and public safety services are constantly being evaluated and improved. Construction of new facilities, expansion of existing routes and modernization of current equipment is ongoing.

In Roswell, the construction of a municipal complex in the 1980s brought public services in North Fulton County into the limelight. The project began with the city's $5 million purchase of the 31-acre Smith estate on Alpharetta and Norcross streets in 1986. One year later, thirteen North Fulton banks united to make low interest "Preservation Special" loans of $53 million to revitalize the 640-acre Roswell Historic District, the only intact example of a pre–Civil War community in the Atlanta area. A preservation plan was developed at that time, identifying the city's 80 historical properties, 39 of which are antebellum, and setting conditions for restoration and future development.

The Historic Preservation Commission was formed to oversee design and landscape of any new development and to guide refurbishing efforts of his-

torically significant sites. Specific zoning regulations and building codes designed to attract new business and regenerate the old town area were put into place.

A design was created to link the northern square, anchored by the Smith Plantation and the future site of the Roswell Municipal complex, with the original town square, anchored by Bulloch Hall and the Roswell Mill.

A $29 million bond referendum was passed in August 1988 to finance construction of the plan which was to include the Roswell City Hall, a civic center, a police station and the city's fifth fire station.

Construction of the $13.5 million, 85,000-square-foot city government complex and adjacent 600-seat cultural center was a critical step in Roswell's "Master Plan" to connect the two historic districts with brick sidewalks and street lights, restoring the village environment created by founding father Roswell King.

The new Roswell City Hall, with its classic Greek revival architecture, red brick facade and gold-domed clock tower has quickly become a landmark in North Fulton. City government offices, once spread throughout the area, are now consolidated and easily accessible to city residents.

The Roswell City Auditorium is nestled into the corner of the 17-acre site next to the new city hall.

*Fireman's Rescue Show, Roswell*

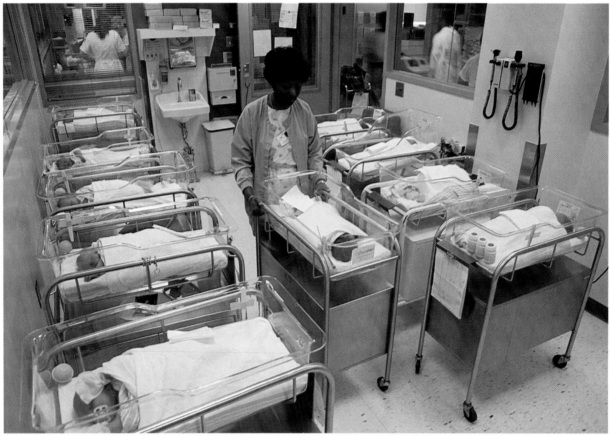

Local groups are already lining up to perform in the 600-seat auditorium which has state-of-the-art lighting and sound systems on the stage, an orchestra pit and balcony seating. The spacious foyer is ideal for receptions and temporary exhibits by local artists.

Roswell residents are also benefiting from the relocation of the city police department to a state-of-the-art facility adjacent to City Hall. The $6.5 million, 48,000-square-foot law enforcement center was built on 3.5 acres at Ellis and Hill streets. It is the city's fastest-growing department, with more than 100 employees servicing 32 square miles.

Although the police headquarters includes both administration space and a full service jail, the building was designed to fit into the architectural specifications of property in the city's 640-acre historic district. The law enforcement headquarters incorporates the most modern equipment available with a spacious floor plan in both the administration and detention center wings. In addition to a computer-simulated firearms training system, a crime lab, photo lab and evidence room have been incorporated into the new complex to assist with criminal investigations.

A five-console communication center occupies the top floor of the administration building to field citywide police, fire and rescue emergency calls. A 911 operator and separate dispatcher handle each call. A large section of the new facility is also devoted to computer-monitored record banks, housed in a dust-free, climate-controlled environment.

Community interest in the new police facility has given rise to the "Citizens Police Academy," a free ten-week course for city residents to experience law enforcement firsthand through lectures, equipment demonstrations and patrol car ride-alongs. The program, which was implemented in 1993, creates the sense of small-town involvement for residents of

Georgia's sixth-largest city.

Equally critical to the city's safety is the volunteer fire department. It is one of 900 fire departments in the state of Georgia, 78 of which are volunteer organizations. Formed in 1935 following a major incident on Elizabeth Way at Canton Street, the city-wide service started with a single two-engine station built in 1937 and since then has grown to five facilities manned by more than 50 professionally trained volunteers servicing a 36-square-mile area. Each of the five stations operates with a captain and ten assigned volunteer firefighters. Hembree Station, the most recent addition, is one of two stations staffed round-the-clock.

In an average year, the Roswell Volunteer Fire and Rescue Department responds to more then 2,400 calls, with an average response time of four minutes. Two-thirds of those calls are for medical emergencies.

Volunteers are required to complete a rigorous 120-hour state training course. Career personnel, including the fire marshall, fire inspectors and a fire-safety educator, have come from the ranks of volunteers and now present fire-safety programs throughout the community. In addition to a standard presentation to all fifth grade elementary school students, trained personnel present programs to local industries, homeowners associations, civic clubs and scout troops in North Fulton.

Local residents enjoy visiting the city's Fire Museum, at the main station on Alpharetta Street. Exhibits include one of the original fire trucks, a 1947 American Ford Pumper, and a working fireman's slide pole. More than 450 North Fulton students visit the museum each month.

Roswell's state-of-the-art equipment, well-trained volunteer force and intensive community education programs have been recognized by the Insurance Services Organization. In recent years fire-safety statistics in both Roswell and Alpharetta, which has a partially volunteer unit, have been acknowledged by the ISO, and both cities have been given better fire-safety ratings.

The opening of two new fire stations, at a cost of $750,000 each, has brought the total number of stations to four in Alpharetta. Facilities were recently added at Maxwell Road adjacent to North Point and at Park Bridge Parkway near Georgia 120 in southeast Alpharetta, to enhance the service provided by the existing stations on Milton Avenue and Windward Parkway.

Mountain Park also has a volunteer fire department which began in the early 1970s. It was started by Jim Busbey, a member of the East Point Volunteer Fire Department, who relocated to Mountain Park. Before, the community had been dependent on Roswell and Alpharetta for fire protection services.

In all of North Fulton, safety as well as environmental concerns have been pressing issues for city governments to address. In keeping with the federal mandate to reduce solid waste by 25 percent or more, North Fulton communities have made an active effort in recent years to recycle.

The North Fulton Recycling Center, which opened in 1989, is the only center in the metro-Atlanta area able to process four different types of plastic, all metals, container glass, four categories of paper, batteries, oil, antifreeze, telephone books and

*Georgia voting*

31

*911 Center*

cardboard. It was selected as one of the nation's most comprehensive programs by the 1990 Earth Day Committee.

Recycling efforts are encouraged by the city's environmental coordinator, who also directs Roswell Clean & Beautiful. Community participation in programs like "Adopt-a-Road," new tree plantings and curbside recycling (introduced in 1992), is very high.

Neighboring Alpharetta was the first North Fulton community to introduce curbside recycling pickup, an active program since July 1990 with a consistent participation rate of 90–94 percent. The city's solid waste management department, created in 1989 to address the critical issue of reducing solid waste, researched the situation thoroughly before contracting with Georgia Waste, a division of Atlanta-based Waste Management, for residential service. The independent service provides separate bins for trash and recyclables, which currently include paper, aluminum and glass. Alpharetta was the first city in the state to offer curbside service to both private homes and apartment complexes.

Curbside recycling has also been a mandatory program since 1990 in the 225 households utilizing city services in Mountain Park.

In unincorporated North Fulton County, many local residents use the Sandy Springs Recycling Center, which opened at a new site on Morgan Falls Road in August 1992. In addition to the standard recycling equipment, the center has a unique four-tiered composting display constructed by Fulton County Extension Service master gardeners. The exhibit, made possible by donations from stores in the community, encourages residents to begin home composting, in order to keep pace with the state mandate to remove lawn clippings from the central waste stream by 1996.

Residents may also recycle newspapers, glass,

32

*Concert on the Square, Roswell*

aluminum cans, magazines and corrugated cardboard boxes at the Morgan Falls facility, though plastic goods are not yet accepted.

Environmental concerns are often a team effort in North Fulton County, where residents will work together to remedy a situation. "Help the Hooch," a river cleanup program held each spring, brings together members of Sandy Springs/North Fulton Clean & Beautiful for a joint effort. The annual Chattahoochee River Awareness Day includes educational programs by National Park Service rangers, wetlands ecology programs and hands-on cleanup of the river banks.

One of the most active North Fulton chapters of Keep America Beautiful is the Alpharetta Clean & Beautiful Commission. More than 18,000 volunteers are committed to the organization, which promotes numerous ongoing projects and clean-up efforts around the city. Members are involved in education, beautification, waste reduction and innovative recycling of items like paint and batteries.

Projects like Adopt-a-Highway, Project Ripple and Project "Saint-Paint" provide a substantial savings to the city because volunteers, rather than city employees, are working to keep the community clean. Project Ripple is enticing thousands of curious North Fulton environmentalists to participate in ongoing water and stream monitoring projects along the banks of Big Creek and Foe Killer Creek in Alpharetta.

The project was initially funded by a $24,000 grant from the Georgia Department of Natural Resources and is directed toward the streams with the heaviest impact on the Chattahoochee River. Since the program's creation in August, 1991, at least 23 streams linked to the Chattahoochee River have been adopted by schools, business organizations and civic groups.

Six water-quality training workshops are held annually at the Environmental Education Center in Alpharetta to acquaint newcomers with the basic know-how for local stream monitoring. Interested volunteers are encouraged to attend these sessions and learn how to use a biotic index to count species living in the stream, measure the chemical balance of the water and monitor physical aspects of the stream and its environs. After attending a workshop, participants are asked to adopt a stream segment which they will observe, clean up and chemically monitor.

Through project "Saint-Paint," latex and acrylic paint donated by residents is recycled into neutral colors which are then given to local charities.

*High school teacher, Dr. Steve Terry*

*Recycling Center, Sandy Springs*

The Alpharetta Environmental Education Center houses an extensive collection of learning resources, pre-arranged lesson plans for all grade levels and "green" videos, to provide North Fulton educators with the research materials to introduce environment-friendly information in the classroom.

City funds and private grants have enabled the creation of the "Green School," an environmental approach to education which has been introduced in Alpharetta schools, reaching more than 10,000 students, staff and parents. The Alpharetta city government has joined forces with an active core of volunteers to educate these people and help keep their portion of North Fulton green.

In recent years Fulton County has also worked to enhance the infrastructure of North Fulton, specifically focusing on water and sewage treatment and facilities. The Fulton County Public Works Department is in the midst of a multi-phase $60 million overhaul of North Fulton sewage lines, including construction of a state-of-the-art $10 million pumping station on Riverside Drive in Roswell. Expansion

of the Big Creek waste-water treatment plant will double the capacity of existing facilities.

Other county- and statewide moves have helped to expand public transportation and the highway system in North Fulton to better service the needs of the rapidly growing community. The continued commercial and residential development along the Georgia 400 corridor has led to increased demand for improved roadways and easier access to MARTA, the Atlanta-based bus and rapid-rail system.

MARTA has provided extensive bus service throughout North Fulton for several decades, including a central park-and-ride facility at Abernathy Road in Sandy Springs.

A second North Fulton park-and-ride site came on line with the opening of the Mansell Road interchange on Georgia 400 in 1992. Mansell Road is one of the Georgia Department of Transportation's only cooperative efforts utilizing funds from both the public and private sector. In addition to providing greater access to Georgia 400 for

*Walk America, Roswell City Hall*

North Fulton residents, the interchange alleviates the congestion on nearby Holcomb Bridge Road and provides greater visibility for the area's growing retail complex at North Point.

Commuter congestion in North Fulton was most profoundly affected by the opening of the 6.25-mile extension of Georgia 400, connecting I-285 with I-85 through Buckhead. After years of opposition by community organizations, the $274 million toll-road extension was completed in 1993.

By mid-1988 the Federal Highway Administration and the Georgia Department of Transportation Board had approved construction of the six-lane limited-access highway with a MARTA rail line in the center median. Government officials and area business leaders determined that the long-range solution to the increasing traffic north of Atlanta rested with the Buckhead connection and effective implementation of MARTA.

The Georgia 400 Extension is the first Toll Pilot Project in the country. Windshield-mounted cards are scanned by radio waves and then electronically recorded in a quarter of a second at each toll collection point. The $274 million construction cost for the extension was split between the federal government, the state of Georgia and the Toll Authority. Based on future usage projections, the bonds will be paid off in twenty years and the toll will be discontinued.

Projections by the Department of Transportation conclude that 166,900 vehicles will travel through Buckhead each day by the year 2010 and 98,600 of these cars will be on Georgia 400.

Clearly North Fulton commuters are on the move, living on the cutting edge of MARTA's innovative plans to take Atlanta's public transportation system into the next century.

Future plans call for expansion of the northern line, with rail stations opening along the DeKalb County-Fulton County line at Medical Center and Dunwoody. The long-range plan calls for the extension of the rapid-rail system to Dunwoody to be completed by 1996 and eventually expand as far north as North Springs by 2004.

Construction of the Buckhead, Dunwoody and Medical Center Stations is currently underway and will be completed prior to the Olympic games in 1996. The Dunwoody station will be located adjacent to Perimeter Mall and have a 600-car parking lot as well as five bus-bays. Overflow parking will be handled by the existing park-and-ride facility on Abernathy Road in Sandy Springs.

According to the North Line Extension Project Report issued by MARTA in May 1991, appropriations of federal funds in the amount of $82.5 million have been set aside for construction on the northern line.

Population forecasts by the Atlanta Regional Commission show that the north-central section of the metro area will experience a 191 percent growth rate, jumping from a population of 148,000 in 1980 to 431,000 in 2010.

In November 1992, MARTA received a $62 million federal grant to finance construction of the north line segment from the Medical Center to the Dunwoody Station. Current plans call for an aerial structure for the 1.14-mile segment between the two stations.

Several other transportation-based changes are waiting in the wings until construction begins on the northern line. Plans include roadway adjustments, expansions and improvements to help ease the stress and congestion of commuting.

MARTA currently relies on a "feeder bus system" in North Fulton County, with bus routes running throughout the community and from the two central park-and-ride lots to the rail station at Lenox Square. Northsiders are able to reach destinations around Atlanta and Hartsfield International Airport easily via rail connections on MARTA.

# North Fulton County Schools

◆

In every corner of America, education has become a lifeline to the future for our nation's youth. In North Fulton County the commitment to quality education is testimony to the communitywide goal of a better standard of living.

Superior facilities, innovative programs and motivated educators, linked with a finely tuned support network of parents and members of the local business community, create an environment where students will strive to succeed.

In both the public school system and in North Fulton's abundance of private facilities, the challenge of providing a high-quality education is being met with excellence.

The Fulton County school system serves 46,000 students who live outside the city limits of Atlanta, including students from Sandy Springs and the surrounding unincorporated areas, as well as students in the incorporated cities of Alpharetta, Roswell and Mountain Park.

All Fulton County schools are accredited by the Southern Association of Colleges and Schools and the Georgia Accrediting Commission. A comprehensive program of instruction and related services are offered for all students, including the developmentally delayed and intellectually gifted. Every facility offers a full range of extracurricular activities, including highly competitive athletic, academic and cultural pursuits. All schools are air-conditioned and carpeted. Specialized art, music and physical education facilities are available at all grade levels, and all schools have been wired for a schoolwide computer network.

Preschool programs are available for handicapped students beginning at age three. Kindergarten readiness programs are also available for certain four-year-olds (identified early as in need), and in all Fulton County schools kindergarten is a full-day program.

More than 70 percent of Fulton County high school graduates continue in postsecondary education programs, and in North Fulton high schools that figure is closer to 90 percent.

The Fulton County School Board is governed by a seven-member board which is elected by districts, four of whom represent greater North Fulton County. In response to growth in recent years, district 7, in the eastern end of North Fulton County, was added in 1992. The county works with an annual budget of $300 million, of which 70 percent is spent directly on instruction.

The growth in North Fulton County in the last twenty years has been unprecedented and one area of life most clearly impacted is the school system. Through 1997 the Fulton County School Board anticipates spending an estimated $77.1 million on seven new elementary schools north of the Chattahoochee River and one new elementary school in Sandy Springs.

*Education Museum*

*Officer Bob, Roswell North Elementary*

A $245 million construction and renovation project begun by the county in 1987 has already resulted in the addition of several state-of-the-art facilities in the Greater North Fulton area and complete refurbishment of existing structures.

In 1990 the county opened Roswell High School, a $13.5 million facility on King Road to replace the original building which was built to accommodate only 350 students.

In 1991, the $11.5 million Chattahoochee High School was completed in Alpharetta, drawing students from the former Crestwood High and a portion of students from the existing Milton High. Standard at both facilities are computer laboratories with network capability in each classroom, comprehensive media centers, athletic facilities, music, art and special education suites.

Following the opening of these new facilities in 1991, Sandy Springs Middle School was moved to the former Crestwood High School building. Students in grades six through eight, living in the geographic area from the Chattahoochee River south to the Atlanta city limits, attend either Ridgeview or Sandy Springs Middle School.

High schools for grades nine through twelve in that same zone of Fulton County are Riverwood or North Springs. On the elementary level, the students in Sandy Springs attend one of four schools for kindergarten through fifth grade: Heards Ferry, High Point, Spalding Drive or Woodland.

Unique programs and diverse student bodies set each of these schools apart. For several years, Spalding Drive Elementary has been the only school in Georgia offering the Jasper Project to fifth graders. The program, which was developed in conjunction with Vanderbilt University and Coca-Cola, encourages students to use computers and video disc players to solve mathematical problems.

Equally impressive is the diverse student body at High Point Elementary, where 44 percent of the 817 students represent twenty different foreign countries.

North of the Chattahoochee River, Fulton County students attend one of 12 elementary schools: Alpharetta, Barnwell, Crabapple Crossing, Dolvin, Esther Jackson, Findley Oaks, Lake Windward, New Prospect, Medlock Bridge, Mimosa, Mountain Park or Roswell North.

This section of the county has experienced

40

tremendous growth in recent years and the school system is rapidly expanding to meet the surging demands of the residents. Elementary school enrollment increased almost 20 percent between 1990 and 1992, jumping from 8,394 students to 9,978.

Two new elementary schools were completed for the 1993–94 academic year, New Prospect Elementary at Georgia 400 and Kimball Bridge, and Findley Oaks Elementary at Findley Road near the Standard Club in Alpharetta. The new facilities will provide additional classroom space for 1,624 elementary students and cost the county $15.4 million to construct.

On the middle school level, students north of the Chattahoochee River attend Crabapple, Haynes Bridge, Holcomb Bridge and Taylor Road middle schools where enrollment was 4,494 students for the 1992–1993 academic year.

The middle school curriculum is comprised of student advisement, interdisciplinary studies, exploratory courses and physical education. Each student begins the day with a 25-minute advisement period followed by academic studies in language arts, mathematics, science and social studies.

Students also take six-week intervals of exploratory programs in art, music, family resource management, industrial arts, keyboarding, drama, journalism, computer utilization, careers and the basics of Spanish and French.

Chattahoochee, Milton, Roswell and Independence high schools provide instruction for Fulton County students living north of the Chattahoochee, in grades nine through twelve. The vocational program, offered in-depth at Milton High School, consists of business and marketing education, family resource management and diversified technology courses.

In order to graduate, all high school students must take a core curriculum of English, social studies, science, mathematics, health and physical education and keyboarding. Additional requirements are necessary for students participating in a college preparatory or vocational program.

On the high school level, Fulton County schools work to meet the diverse needs of the student body. Independence High School in Roswell offers an open-campus program for approximately 250 stu-

dents who can profit from a less traditional approach to academics and a more flexible schedule. Working at their own pace, students receive grades when they have completed the coursework. There are no athletics or extracurricular activities and students must provide their own transportation. Child-care services are available.

Two Greater North Fulton area high schools, Riverwood and North Springs, are also home to the Magnet Program for students interested in an academic concentration in either International Studies or Mathematics/Science. Participating students must first complete the core curriculum courses and maintain a grade average of C or higher in all academic courses.

*Roswell High marching band*

41

*Epstein School*

cal ingredient in the success of the Greater North Fulton area schools. In 1991, three schools—Mimosa Elementary, Crabapple Middle and Crestwood High—received the highest honors given by the Georgia PTA. Structured organizations like the PTSA at each school, as well as grassroots groups like the Chattahoochee Area Advisory Board, have a positive impact on policies in education. Parents from the six elementary schools that feed into Chattahoochee High recently joined forces in a team effort to heighten the awareness of public officials to the critical issues in the schools.

Another project spearheaded by concerned parents and community leaders is the Roswell High School Foundation, a group involved in a fundraising effort to finance construction of additional athletic facilities and fields at the high school's new site on King Road. Roswell traditionally has some of the area's most competitive teams on the AAAA-level.

The creative approach to education in Fulton County is evidenced by the Teaching Museum North, a multi-purpose facility which opened in North Fulton in 1992. If the glossy heart-pine floors in the restored Roswell Elementary School on Mimosa Boulevard could speak, they would tell the tale of Roswell as an old mill village, little changed through most of the 20th century. They would tell the story of life during the Depression, the rapid growth since the 1970s and the recent transformation to a unique teaching museum for area students. Now, the once-quiet halls of the abandoned school building are again pulsing with excitement and life, with fascinating exhibits staged in classrooms and hallways.

Restored in a joint effort by the city of Roswell and the Fulton County Board of Education, the school was designed to celebrate the history of education and present it to students in a meaningful way with hands-on experiences.

Roswell Elementary, an educational site since 1838, and North Avenue Elementary in Hapeville, designed by renowned architect Phillip Shutze, were selected for identical museum projects at the north and south ends of Fulton County.

Children from every grade level can enjoy the

Each year, the Georgia Department of Education selects an elementary, middle and high school from each congressional district as a State School of Excellence. In 1993, Haynes Bridge Middle School was recognized with this honor.

Other middle schools which received this honor in the past include Sandy Springs Middle School, a two-time recipient, and Crabapple Middle School, a National School of Excellence. In the past, the Georgia Department of Education has also named Esther Jackson, Dolvin, Heards Ferry and Roswell North elementary schools as Georgia Schools of Excellence. Dolvin was also honored by the U.S. Department of Education as a Blue Ribbon School and in 1991 Mimosa Elementary School was honored as having the most outstanding PTA in Georgia.

Parental and community involvement is a criti-

creative historic interpretations in each exhibit area. From its storytellers in period costume to reenactments of the bread lines and bleak financial times of the 1930s, the museum is a wonderful tool to enhance traditional educational techniques.

Original exhibits include a Writer's Corner, featuring a mural of photos and works by 23 Georgia authors; an authentic log cabin which recreates life in Georgia during the 1870s; and a political science room with an unusual collection of artifacts and memorabilia relating to Georgia in the 1930s.

Three displays completed in 1993 include a "toy" attic, Historic Women wall mural by local artist Gary Bannister, and a Roswell Mill diorama by model-railroad buff Kelly Taylor. The toy attic features a collection of antique toys and books on loan from Jackie Littlefield, assistant principal of High Point Elementary, as well as other pieces donated by members of the community. The hallway mural by Mr. Bannister traces the women's movement through large cut-out figures of important women in American history, and the glass-enclosed diorama accurately portrays life in the Roswell Mill village from 1880–1890.

Fulton County is one of three school systems in the United States selected to participate in the Smithsonian Institute/National Faculty program which provides access to traveling exhibits for the Teaching Museum. The project promotes museum literacy through a partnership with the school system which includes the exchange of exhibits and learning materials. Fulton County teachers are also able to participate in hands-on training at the Washington, D.C. facility which will enable them to incorporate a multicultural perspective into their classroom presentation.

Although the primary focus of the Teaching Museum is students, the community plays an active role by providing volunteers and docents. Many programs—including the Roswell Historic District walking tours for fifth and eighth graders and the cultural seminars for high school students—rely on local artists, writers and members of the North Fulton community.

The community has also played a crucial role in the formation of Greater North Fulton Education 2000 Inc., an umbrella organization for groups that

address educational needs and encourage volunteer support for education. The effort is overseen by a board of directors comprised of leaders in business, education and government.

Greater North Fulton Education 2000, Inc. was created to help the North Fulton schools focus on the six nationwide goals established by America 2000. The plan challenges American educators to: achieve a high school graduation rate of at least 90 percent, make U.S. students first in the world in science and math achievement, achieve a drug- and violence-free school environment, guarantee that every child comes to school ready to learn, insure that all students learn to use their minds well in challenging subject matters, and finally, insure that every adult will be a literate, skilled, responsible citizen.

Two projects already underway are "Project Soar" and the "Best Kids" program. "Project Soar"

*Grade School Field Day*

started as a mentoring program for students at the Independence High School and the Cottage School in Roswell, and is now being expanded to offer mentoring and tutoring to all secondary students in North Fulton.

The "Best Kids" program, which is jointly sponsored by Kroger and Greater North Fulton Education 2000, Inc., provides parenting-skills workshops, kindergarten readiness programs and

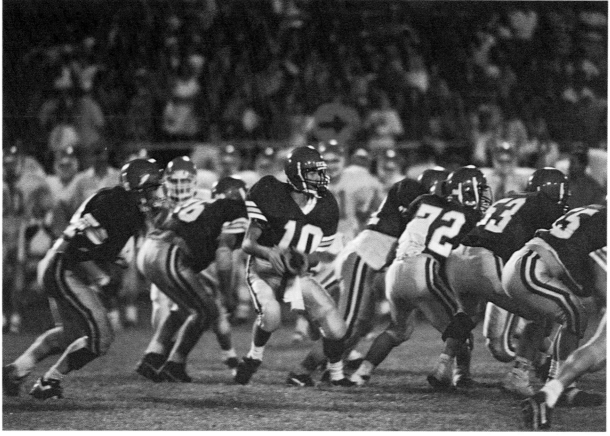

*Roswell High football game*

creative activities for school-aged children on subjects like substance abuse, safety, self-esteem and cultural awareness. This program was cited by the Georgia Partnership for Excellence in Education, a statewide organization of educators and business leaders interested in improving education on a statewide level.

Two education-based marketing campaigns have sprung from this program: "Bringing Learning Home," which stresses the importance of parental involvement, and "Hire the Graduate," a graduation employment incentive package available through local businesses.

There are currently more than 100 businesses participating in the Partners in Education Program in North Fulton. The level of involvement varies but many business partners are responsible for implementing exciting new educational experiences for the students.

At Roswell North Elementary School, Kroger, the Partner in Education, has set up a "Mini Store for Learning," fully equipped with a cash register, money, shelved items and shopping baskets. Students, who role-play as employees and customers, get firsthand experience with mathematics and business instruction.

Other community involvement in the Fulton County school system includes the community education department, which offers educational, recreational and job-related classes for county citizens throughout the year for a nominal fee. More than 20,000 Fulton County citizens participate in the programs each year, selecting from at least 75 courses each quarter in a variety of topics like computer training, foreign languages, child-care certification, financial planning and investing.

Pre-school programs (ages 3–5), private and church-affiliated schools, and higher education opportunities abound for North Fulton residents.

# Jessica McFarland

From the optimum vantage of a home on Alpharetta's Main Street, Milton High School senior Jessica McFarland has experienced the growth of North Fulton firsthand.

Her experience, like that of many natives of the vibrant community, exemplifies the area's commitment to both preserving history and encouraging progress.

The names and places have changed but many of the faces have remained the same in the daily life of the ambitious 17-year-old, a third-generation native of the quaint historic town, which has been one of the fastest-growing areas in the nation during the last decade.

"Growing up in a small town has been a very positive experience. It means that everyone knows you and is supportive of you, because they knew your parents or grandparents," she says. "Even with the development in recent years, in some parts of Alpharetta, it is as if time stood still and it is still a small town."

Like many of North Fulton's earliest families, the McFarlands were landowners and farmers for several generations, helping to shape the face of the community from the mid-1900s through present day. Jessica's grandparents both attended school in the original Milton High School building in the early 1940s, when classes for grades kindergarten through twelfth grade were all under one roof, and helped to develop organizations like the Future Farmers of America, which is still in existence today.

At Milton High School, the growth of Alpharetta has resulted in both tangible changes, like construction of modern facilities, and intangible changes, like the development of a diverse student body, according to the talented young woman, who has found her niche as editor of the school newspaper and literary magazine.

"Some people have grown up and are content in the small town while others are headed in different directions," she says. "I've saved special things like the poem the mailman wrote about my grandfather when he died, and now it's time to experience other places."

# ECONOMIC DEVELOPMENT
# IN NORTH FULTON

◆

As growth continues to surge north on the Georgia 400 corridor, the abundance of affordable land, high quality of life and educated labor force in the Greater North Fulton area is attracting major national and international corporations. In addition to altering the skyline, these corporations bring economic stability, employment opportunities and support for community organizations to North Fulton.

Controlled growth in the commercial real-estate market has resulted in the development of two distinct environments—the pre-existing contemporary office parks at the perimeter adjacent to Sandy Springs, and the lush, sprawling complexes for build-to-suit development in Alpharetta. By offering both, North Fulton has an unlimited supply of space to meet the specifications of any enterprise looking to relocate.

There have been several key players in the commercial real-estate development of the Georgia 400 corridor, including Cousins Properties; Carter & Associates; Mobil Land Development; Johnson Development; Jim Cowart, Inc.; Technology Park, Inc.; and, most recently, Homart Development Company.

Carter & Associates has developed or provided real-estate consulting services for ten projects totaling almost two million square feet, including impressive corporate campuses for Kimberly-Clark, AT&T

and Contel. Carter & Associates also developed a facility on State Bridge Road for Siemens Energy & Automation, an internationally owned supplier of full-line electrical equipment and systems.

The 400 corridor has always been attractive to companies wishing to acquire large tracts of undeveloped land and do a build-to-suit facility. In 1981, Kimberly-Clark selected a site along Georgia 400. Today, the division headquarters on Holcomb Bridge Road in Roswell consists of 460,000 square feet in six buildings in a parklike, suburban setting.

Carter has also worked with communications giant AT&T, who initially had a small land holding in Windward. The property was expanded to almost 200 acres and a custom facility was designed and built for Contel.

From an economic perspective, North Fulton is a recession-proof community with attractive demographics for both small and large retailers. Studies by local agencies estimate that there are more than 200,000 potential shoppers in the North Fulton trade area with the metro area's highest average household income of $63,000.

These statistics have generated the commercial boom along Roswell Road in Sandy Springs, supporting the "Mom and Pop" shops that give North Fulton its charm, and attracting national developers who have created a large retail complex in the heart of the area.

*Siemens Corporate Headquarters, Alpharetta*

*Church raising, Roswell*

As growth continues to surge north on the Georgia 400 corridor, economic trends paint a bright picture for North Point Mall, the 1.15-million-square-foot regional mall at Georgia 400 and Haynes Bridge Road.

The mega-complex, which opened in October 1993, has five anchor department stores, 150 retail shops and restaurants, an enclosed 30-foot working carousel and a full-scale, on-site customer service facility.

The high-tech design, complete with 85-foot-high continuous skylights that measure the length of three football fields, is only one of the many unique aspects of the 100-acre development by Homart Development Company and JMB/Federated. Although it is the first Atlanta mall for Homart, the firm handles 29 other shopping complexes around the country.

Unusual retailers, many new to the Atlanta market, enhance the shopping opportunities found at the five main anchor stores: Sears, Rich's, JCPenney, Mervyn's and Lord & Taylor.

Exciting "one-of-a-kind" stores like a Braves Clubhouse Store, The Great Train Store and Ozone! Hi-Tech Electronics—a gadget gallery owned by former Atlanta Braves center fielder Otis Nixon—are sure to attract a steady stream of retail traffic.

Seventeen "eateries" including Mick's, Cinnabon, Cajun & Grill and Le Petit Bistro, offer quick snacks or full-scale dining to shoppers in the 40,500-square-foot food court that has seating for 50 on the outdoor patio as well as an indoor dining area.

Next to the food court, a fully operational 30-foot carousel entertains weary shoppers, young or old. The hand-painted merry-go-round with its brightly colored animals, is the tallest piece ever manufactured by Fabricon Carousel Company, the New York-based supplier. The unusual attraction, which can accommodate 38 people, is enclosed in a huge glass atrium visible from the parking lot and plays calliope music during operation.

Market analysts predict brisk traffic at North Point based on household income figures and population trends in the North Fulton community.

From 1980 to 1990, the average income of households within ten miles of the new regional center rose 78 percent to $72,000 and the population more than doubled to 335,000. For potential retailers, those demographics translate into aggressive trade figures and steady sales.

The mall is just a portion of Cousins Properties' master plan for North Point, which includes sites for development of banks, restaurants, hotels, strip shopping-centers and office space.

More than 320 acres surrounding the mall are owned by Cousins Properties, a leading player in the Atlanta commercial real-estate market, who sold the original 100-acre mall site to Homart Development. Cousins has developed more than 20 million square feet of retail and corporate space since its formation in 1960.

North Point Parkway, a six-lane north-south roadway paralleling Georgia 400, and the expansion of Haynes Bridge Road east of Georgia 400 to a six-lane thoroughfare with turn lanes and a median, were completed as a result of the project, which has been on the drawing board since 1986.

Build-out plans for the complex include a major office component, retail "power center" and outparcels for banks, restaurants and support stores. Cousins/New Market Development Company, a division of Cousins Properties, has developed Mansell Crossing and North Point Market, two "power centers" already in place. Final build-out on projects in the 500-acre site will bring the retail space at North Point close to the original projections of one million square feet.

While crowds of shoppers descend on the new mega-complex, the shopping hubs of Sandy Springs and small retailers grouped in commercial pockets in Roswell and Alpharetta continue to thrive because of their quaint settings and unique merchandise.

*Harry's Farmers Market*

49

*North Point Mall grand opening*

The original North Fulton Chamber of Commerce was formed in 1972, with the help of the U.S. Chamber in Washington D.C., as a permanent, positive voice to provide business counseling and address other issues unique to the North Fulton community.

In June 1992, the 350-member Sandy Springs Chamber of Commerce united forces with the 900-member North Fulton Chamber to create the Greater North Fulton Chamber of Commerce. Because Sandy Springs has existing commercial buildings and Alpharetta has land ready for development, the merger has created a broad service base for businesses considering North Fulton. From its beginning as a round-table discussion led by Roswell architect Zachary Henderson, the organization has mushroomed to 1,250 members.

The Chamber meets the needs of any size organization—from local entrepreneurs to Fortune 500 companies based in North Fulton—through ongoing networking sessions, an annual trade show and community outreach efforts. The Chamber's leadership program targets a select group of community leaders who attend a nine-month series of workshops, demonstrations and projects focusing on community awareness and leadership skills.

In addition to uniting leadership teams, the newly formed organization has merged committees to address areas like membership recruiting, small-business services, economic development of the community and educational services for members.

The Chamber has also been the impetus for the annual Colors of North Fulton Festival, a six-week-long business and cultural celebration featuring road races, performances by local dance, theatrical and musical ensembles, the AT&T Challenge, the Crabapple Antique Festival, the Roswell Antebellum Festival, Taste of Alpharetta, semi-annual concerts by the Atlanta Symphony Orchestra, and arts festivals on the town square and special entertainment for children.

Tourism is a growing economic enterprise in North Fulton. Southern hospitality and old-world charm are two important selling features in the highly competitive struggle for Atlanta's tourist dollars, which is why the city of Roswell recently invested $100,000 to revamp the former city hall

*North Point Mall construction*

and the surrounding grounds into an inviting visitor's center in the heart of the town's historic district.

The facility is operated by the Historic Roswell District Owners & Business Association Inc., an umbrella organization of 250 area business owners, property owners and organizations involved with the historic district.

Maps and pamphlets are available free of charge at the center, providing information on sights in the town square, the historic stretch of businesses along Canton Street and the bustling complex of merchants and activities in the Roswell Mill.

In addition to general information on the area, the visitor's center actively promotes citywide events like the annual Concert Series on the Square sponsored by the city, the Roswell Mill Concert Series, productions by local theater groups and numerous other festivals.

Antique shops and upscale clothing stores are also popular stops for tourists visiting Roswell's historic town square, and part of the Southern small-town mystique. One particularly unique shop, The Sophisticated Swine, attracts shoppers from all corners of Atlanta to browse through the trendy boutique and visit with the resident pig, Sophie.

The 35-pound Julianna pig has been adopted as the town's unofficial mascot by many North Fulton shoppers who head to the upscale emporium to find unusual decorative items for the home, snazzy ladies' apparel and accessories, tempting Georgia edibles and quality gift items.

Hobbit Hall, a children's bookstore near the town square, is another one-of-a-kind Roswell retail venture. The store, which opened in May 1992, was originally a vacant home on Bulloch Avenue in Roswell. Owners Anne Ginkel and Bill Crawford completely remodeled the interior but maintained the cozy architectural style and charm. Renovations included creating an inviting reading nook on a boardwalk over a fish pond at the entrance, building a large wooden playhouse in the enclosed back garden and updating the basement into classroom/programming space.

North Fulton families regularly participate in activities sponsored by Hobbit Hall such as storytelling sessions, visits by children's authors, special holiday celebrations and reading enrichment programs. Frequent visitors at the quaint Roswell store include Carmen Agra Deedy, creator of the Atlanta Storytelling Festival, and Hobbit Hall next-door neighbor Emily Dolvin.

*Computone Communication Adapters Manufacturing*

*Winter snowstorm*

# GREATER NORTH FULTON CHAMBER OF COMMERCE

One of the fastest-growing and successful chambers in Georgia, the Greater North Fulton Chamber of Commerce (GNFCC) has been in business to promote business for over 20 years. A product of the June 1992 merger of the Sandy Springs and North Fulton chambers of commerce, the GNFCC now services more than 1,300 business members from Alpharetta, Mountain Park, Roswell, Sandy Springs and Unincorporated North Fulton County.

The primary mission of the Greater North Fulton Chamber of Commerce is to promote North Fulton's business and professional community, and continue the tremendous growth and success of the past decade. The chamber works continuously with all levels of government to support the infrastructure needed to maintain North Fulton's high quality of life. The GNFCC has played a key role in projects such as the Mansell Road construction, revitalization plans for Roswell, Sandy Springs, Alpharetta and Fulton County, and various other public-private partnerships that have benefited the business and residential communities within the Greater

*Sales Meeting*

North Fulton area.

Chamber committees also work to solve issues that affect North Fulton County. One of the Chamber's largest organizations, Greater North Fulton Education 2000, Inc., works to promote life-long learning and improve educational opportunities in the area. Established in 1993, the non-profit foundation has over 100 members comprised of educators, businesses, civic organizations, and elected officials. Some of the projects GNF Education 2000 is involved in include a mentoring program, special after-school programs for "at risk" children and programs promoting worker literacy. The Chamber's year-long Leadership North Fulton program teaches the area's "up and coming" leaders about challenges North Fulton faces. Education is extremely important to the Chamber and area businesses because quality education provides quality employees, and draws quality companies to North Fulton.

Small businesses comprise nearly 85 percent of the area's business demographics, and the Chamber has a well-established small business work area which develops programs and opportunities for that diverse group. Timely seminars, monthly networking events, affordable health insurance, and an annual trade show are some of the benefits provided to Chamber members to give them the edge to compete in today's competitive business world. Free small business counseling at the Chamber offices, compliments of Georgia State and University of Georgia's Small Business Development Centers, makes opening or expanding a business easier, too.

Several large annual events are also created to benefit the communities within North Fulton County. The annual Golf & Tennis Outing raises money for three scholarships awarded each spring to graduating high school seniors. The month long, community-wide "Colors Celebration," created by the Chamber in 1991, brings over 150,000 visitors to the area and makes local business cash registers ring. A semi-annual concert in North Fulton by the Atlanta Symphony Orchestra provides residents with free entertainment by a world-class musical group. EXPO, the Chamber's annual trade event, attracts over 1,000 potential customers for Chamber member exhibitors.

In order to maintain and enhance the area's quality of life, the GNFCC established a cultural and community affairs division in 1992. In 1993, the organization became partners with Fulton County and succeeded in acquiring 19.5 acres along the Chattahoochee River to be used for a Fine Arts Center planned to open in 1996. The Chamber also played a key role in the establishment of Fulton Arts North, an arts advocacy organization guided by the Fulton County Arts Council. Another Chamber-supported organization, the Greater North Fulton Civic Roundtable, provides a forum for local residents and businesses to meet with elected officials and discuss issues of common import.

Formed in the spring of 1991, the Greater North Fulton Chamber's Economic Development Council works to promote high-quality development and redevelopment, raises funds to market the area, and continually prospects for potential new business moves to the Greater North Fulton area. Every time a business opens its doors, North Fulton's tax base is expanded. Increased revenues allow local government to build parks and recreational facilities, improve their educational systems, upgrade their infrastructure, and keep taxes low. This benefits both businesses and the residents of North Fulton County.

There is one simple reason why the communities within North Fulton County are the fastest growing in the country. It's the best place to work and live in the United States!

*North Point Mall*

**AT&T**

*A*T&T brings a long and rich history to North Fulton. AT&T was incorporated in 1885, and traces its lineage to Alexander Graham Bell and his invention of the telephone in 1876. As parent company of the former Bell System, AT&T's primary mission was to provide universal telephone service to virtually everyone in the United States. In its first 40 years, AT&T established subsidiaries and allied companies in more than a dozen other countries. It sold these interests in 1925 and focused on achieving its mission in the U.S. It did, however, continue to provide international long distance service.

AT&T recently expanded its North Fulton operation with a two-building, 315,000-square-foot facility addition. These new buildings, opened in the first quarter of 1992, complement the five previously constructed ones, which were built in 1985.

The entire 265-acre tract in Windward, located on North Point Parkway in Alpharetta, houses over 3,000 employees. These individuals help comprise AT&T's total metro-Atlanta workforce, second only to its workforce in New Jersey.

The way AT&T treats its employees and directs its philanthropic support influences its reputation and touches thousands of communities. It is a responsibility taken very seriously.

The AT&T Foundation, the company's principal vehicle for corporate philanthropy, makes grants in support of education, health care, human services and cultural organizations. In 1992, the Foundation contributed $33.2 million through 846 direct grants and donations that matched the personal contributions of employees and retirees. About half of the Foundation's budget is directed to education.

AT&T is firmly established in North Fulton corporate participation efforts. The company participates in many local initiatives, including the Coalition for a Drug Free North Fulton, Leadership North Fulton, local high schools' Youth Motivation Day, Junior Achievement's Project Business, and the North Fulton Chamber Service. The AT&T Pioneers, a service organization of AT&T employees, also participates in many charitable activities.

AT&T has more than 308,000 employees, with approximately 53,000 working outside the United States. Two major unions represent AT&T employees: The Communication Workers of America represents 95,000 AT&T people, while 23,000 are represented by the International Brotherhood of Electrical Workers. In 1992, AT&T and its unions negotiated a three-year contract that marked a new level of union-management cooperation.

AT&T often appears in lists of best companies

Photo Courtesy of AT&T

The Bell System was dissolved at the end of 1983 with AT&T's divestiture of the Bell telephone companies. Today, AT&T operates worldwide (over 120 countries) in competitive, high-technology markets, with only its long distance services remaining under government regulation. With 2.3 million registered share owners, AT&T is the most widely held stock in America.

to work for. Often cited are its ground-breaking Work and Family Program, its support of diversity in the work place and its training programs. Developed with its unions, AT&T's Work and Family Program provides referral services and funding for community-based child- and elder-care programs and other policies and options to help employees balance the demands of work and family.

AT&T has a strong commitment to good environmental performance, with environmental goals that call for phase-out of CFC emissions from manufacturing operations, elimination of reportable toxic air emissions, reduction of manufacturing process waste disposal, increased recycling of our waste paper and reduction in our use of paper.

AT&T's progress has been dramatic. AT&T factories have reduced use of CFC emissions by 86 percent, reduced reportable toxic air emissions by 81 percent, and reduced manufacturing waste by 49 percent. The company is recycling about 60 percent of its wastepaper (about 61 million pounds annually), and has increased its use of recycled paper significantly. In 1992, it reduced paper consumption by 10 percent, or 3,000 tons.

AT&T is dedicated to being the world's best at bringing people together—giving them easy access to each other and to the information and services they want and need—anytime, anywhere. AT&T is proud to be part of the growing North Fulton community.

# AHLSTROM RECOVERY INC.

The United States is the world's largest manufacturer of paper. Each year, paper is used to publish 2 billion books, 350 million magazines, and 24 billion newspapers. It's hard to imagine an "Information Age" without paper.

Manufacturers of paper products are facing monumental issues that challenge their survival in the coming decade, including demands for long-term quality improvement, capital-intense production, and dealing with the environment and the demand for environmentally-friendly products.

Ahlstrom Recovery is helping meet these monumental challenges by engineering and building systems which reclaim chemicals from the pulp and papermaking process and generate power at a significantly lower cost. The result is improved pulp quality and virtually no waste, with minimal environmental impact of the mill's production processes.

A subsidiary of A. Ahlstrom Corporation of Helsinki, Finland, Ahlstrom Recovery can draw upon its parent's 140-year involvement with the forest products industry.

Ahlstrom first began marketing products in North America in 1977 out of Glen Falls, NY. In 1989, Ahlstrom Recovery moved to Roswell to establish its North American headquarters. To date, the company has sold over $500 million worth of chemical recovery equipment in North America and has managed 20 large turnkey projects.

Ahlstrom can take single-source responsibility for all elements of a project—including engineering, sourcing, financing, project management, start-up and commissioning.

Ahlstrom Recovery employs people in the following disciplines: sales, customer service, engineering, project management, procurement, technical support, research and development, and administration. Of this number, 55 percent are degreed engineers. In total, the management team has 160 years experience serving the pulp and paper industry.

Photo Courtesy of Ahlstrom Recovery Inc.

Suppliers who work in concert with their customers are proving to be the standard for success in the coming years. Whether it's improving the environmental efficiency of its products, or creating new high-tech systems, Ahlstrom's solutions build upon a 140-year tradition of innovation. In concert with its customers, Ahlstrom will always apply the best minds to master the fundamentals ever more effectively.

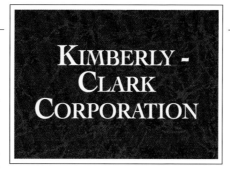

# KIMBERLY - CLARK CORPORATION

In 1872, Kimberly-Clark's founders committed their new company to the principles of quality, service and fair dealing. Today, this commitment remains unchanged. As a leading manufacturer of consumer, paper and health-care products, Kimberly-Clark has come to represent excellence in many highly competitive markets.

From the introduction of Kotex feminine pads and Kleenex facial tissue in the 1920s, to the more recent debut of such products as Huggies disposable diapers and Pull-Ups training pants, Kimberly-Clark has remained at the forefront of technology and product innovation.

Kimberly-Clark is a Fortune 100 company with its world headquarters in Dallas, Texas. Consumer product businesses are based in Neenah, Wisconsin, and nonconsumer products in Roswell, Georgia. Kimberly-Clark employs 49,000 people worldwide, of which 23,000 are in the U.S.

The company's presence in North Fulton County has been and will continue to be a key component of Kimberly-Clark's success. Kimberly-Clark established its office and research facility in Roswell in 1980 to support its rapid growth. The site was expanded in 1982 and 1985 and is headquarters for approximately 1,100 people.

The Roswell facility is headquarters for a number of major business units—the Pulp and Newsprint Sector, Paper and Specialty Products Sector, Service and Industrial Sector and the Professional Health Care and Nonwovens Sector. Roswell is also home for a number of staff units and the nonwovens research and engineering group. The company's proprietary nonwoven materials are used in and provide competitive advantages for many of its consumer and health-care products.

The Roswell operation has also established

Kimberly-Clark as a key player in the local business community, both as a well-regarded employer and as a generous contributor to charitable efforts. Kimberly-Clark is a major supporter of United Way and a variety of organizations that meet cultural and human services needs. The Corporation's commitment extends to employees, who enjoy on-site health care and exercise facilities, educational support, including scholarships for qualified sons and daughters, and support for community involvement.

© Phillip Spears- Creative Sources Photography, Inc.

Kimberly-Clark's success in North America and strong product franchises have led to substantial worldwide expansion. Combining its well-known brand names with its core technologies in fiber, absorbency and nonwovens, Kimberly-Clark's goal is to be recognized as one of the handful of best companies in the world. To achieve this, Kimberly-Clark maintains a commitment to employ the best people, produce and sell the best products and provide the best returns to its stockholders.

## WINDWARD
## A MOBIL LAND COMMUNITY

When an award-winning residential community is designed around top-notch recreational facilities and a state-of-the-art corporate campus, the result is an ideal environment where families can live, work and play.

The result is Windward, a masterfully crafted 3,400-acre planned, mixed-use community, developed around a 195-acre private lake by Mobil Land Development (GA) Corporation in Alpharetta.

As a residential community, Windward offers the finest in traditional and contemporary homes, built by a select group of accomplished custom builders. With 20 distinct neighborhoods catering to individual price and lifestyle needs, Windward has attracted more than 1,200 families since development began in 1983.

Residents enjoy an active lifestyle with diverse recreational opportunities and community-wide organizations like the Windward Garden Club, Windward Women's Club and Retired Men's Club. Families gather regularly at the Windward Sports Park, which offers areas for baseball, football, basketball, picnicking, lakeside docking and boat launching for Windward residents. Annual celebrations like the Fourth of July parade help make the Windward lifestyle unique.

Adjacent to Lake Windward, the centerpiece of the community, is the private membership Windward Lake Club. Sixteen tennis courts, an Olympic-sized swimming pool, a kiddie pool and boat storage areas are available to all members of the full-service facility.

Topping the list of attractions at Windward is The Golf Club of Georgia, a 36-hole private club, created by Fuji Development USA, Ltd. The rolling greens and undulating fairways of the two 18-hole golf courses, which weave throughout the business and residential community, were designed by Arthur Hills. The Lakeside Course has been recognized as one of the top golf courses in the country.

Other features which contribute to the superior quality of life at Windward include important community elements like the Windward Fire Station and Lake Windward Elementary School, one of Fulton County's leading facilities.

Windward's master plan also includes an expansive business community, offering a variety of sites designed to accommodate everything from corporate headquarters to distribution, research and development facilities. The attractive business setting, which currently contains 3 million square feet of office and service space employing over 7,000 people, is already home to AT&T,

Digital Communications Associates, Equifax, UPS, Holiday Inn Worldwide and GE Capital Services Corporation.

Collectively, the Windward business community and residential neighborhoods reflect the commitment to quality and excellence that have become hallmarks at Mobil Land Development. They provide an ideal environment to live, work and play in North Fulton County.

Windward is an equal housing opportunity community.

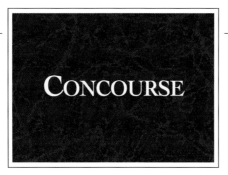

# CONCOURSE

Known as the gateway to North Fulton County, the two 33-story signature towers at Concourse rise as beacons above I-285 and Georgia 400. This 63-acre, mixed-use office complex combines a lush, lakefront setting, dramatic architecture, and the most comprehensive array of amenities found in Atlanta.

© McGee Photography

Concourse began with the vision of bringing together a dynamic blend of the best of both urban and suburban environments. Land acquisition involved negotiating the purchase of a 40-home subdivision, made obsolete by the arrival of two new freeways, located at the intersection of Hammond Drive and Peachtree-Dunwoody Road. After receiving unprecedented county zoning approvals for density, height, and usage, construction began in 1983 on Corporate Center One, an eight-story, 288,000-square-foot office building.

Today, Concourse includes five corporate centers totalling 2.1 million square feet. The mid-rise corporate centers feature soaring atrium lobbies with striking hanging kites or stained glass art. The tower lobbies feature warm granite and glistening marbles with dramatic commissioned oil paintings or wall hangings. Its two towers are the tallest office buildings in suburban Atlanta and were rapidly leased, an indication of their overwhelming success in the north central business district.

Unsurpassed in its amenities, Concourse offers a 371-room Doubletree Hotel, the 80,000-square-foot, world-class Concourse Athletic Club, an on-site KinderCare Learning Center, six restaurants, bank, hair salon, newsstand/sundry shops, travel agencies, gourmet coffee shop, and auto detailing. Each of the two towers has its own concierge, who assists tenants in handling everything from arranging limousine service to purchasing theater tickets.

Concourse successfully combines work and leisure to create a more productive atmosphere. Concourse Athletic Club has been an outstanding success with tenants and surrounding communities. Members enjoy the club's two 2.5-meter indoor and outdoor pools, squash, racquetball and tennis courts, state-of-the-art body-building equipment, and cardiovascular machines. The club's restaurant, Courtside Grille, is a popular eating spot, open to the public for lunch and dinner. The club also features a sports medicine facility.

The on-site KinderCare Learning Center was another way of making it a little easier for Concourse tenants and neighbors to leave home every morning. Now they enjoy the convenience and security of knowing their little ones are close at hand.

An integral part of the community and a popular site for local civic, cultural, and charitable events, Concourse is the choice time and again of companies wanting to generate interest and participation for their events — from lakeside concerts to walk-a-thons and a Vietnam Veterans' Association dedication ceremony.

During the last decade, Concourse has truly set the standard for office development in the central perimeter area, clearly defining the productive work environment demanded by today's busy professionals.

# CITY OF ALPHARETTA

When the *Wall Street Journal* cited Alpharetta as one of 10 up-and-coming "boom" areas in the country recently, it was no surprise. Situated 30 miles north of Atlanta in one of the most dynamic growth corridors in the state, the city is poised to become nothing less than a new urban metropolis.

Alpharetta has come to represent the kind of city that a growing number of Americans want to

live in. It has an endearing small-town flavor that government and citizens strive to preserve. Because the city strives to balance the desires of citizens with the needs of business, Alpharetta has maintained its quality throughout the growth.

Good examples are North Point Mall and two adjacent shopping centers, which opened in 1993 with an estimated 2.4 million square feet of retail, restaurant and entertainment space. Through negotiations with the mall developer, the city spared hundreds of old-growth trees that ring the mall area, making it one of the prettiest malls in the nation. The surrounding area was carefully

zoned to provide a mix of office towers and retail centers, with buffers to protect nearby residential areas.

Near the mall, within a two-mile stretch along Georgia 400, the city expects explosive residential and commercial growth to follow. A new skyline, shaped by high-rise office buildings, hotels, medical facilities and entertainment centers, is likely.

With Alpharetta's high design standards and advanced planning, it's no wonder that the list of landowners in this area reads like a Who's Who of the nation's premier developers: Mobil Land Development, Ross Perot, Cousins Properties, General Electric Capital, Marine Midland Bank, Roger Staubach, Metropolitan Life Insurance, Trammell Crow and Amstar International, to name a few. It's also not surprising that planners predict a population and employment boom to the tune of 55,000 citizens and roughly twice that many jobs in Alpharetta by the year 2010.

Already Alpharetta has competed with cities nationwide to attract corporate giants. Many high-tech firms, such as AT&T, American Honda, Digital Communications Associates, Digital Equipment Corp., Equifax and Siemens, have located in the city. Recently the Southern Baptist Home Mission Board broke ground on a 34-acre site that will serve as their national headquarters.

This type of development will have a ripple effect in Alpharetta's central business district, where businesses will enjoy the added traffic. Plans are being developed to retain the downtown as a vibrant business area. The plan defines a small-town theme which will become a haven of boutiques, shops, restaurants and unique attractions in the town's historic center. The city is also planning a streetscape program to beautify the town with new landscaping, sidewalks, monuments, mini parks and other features.

As with all fast-growing communities, transportation is an issue. Alpharetta has taken a proactive step in financing a $65 million road improvement program. This program will ensure that the system is built now to handle tomorrow's traffic. Today, major roads are becoming divided parkways with beautifully landscaped medians and roadsides designed in harmony with the city's street design standards.

MARTA, the local transit authority, plans to build a rapid-rail station inside Alpharetta's corporate limits within the next decade. This will provide a fast, direct link to Atlanta's central business district and Hartsfield International Airport.

Alpharetta's vision of transportation goes beyond cars. It also includes a plan for a citywide network of pedestrian trails and bikeways. The city's ambitious plan has already won the state's largest per capita grant of federal transportation monies for such a project, approximately $1 million.

Linked to this system is a proposed five-mile greenway through the center of the city's office district, which will forever preserve the beautiful terrain and wetlands along Big Creek. This system will provide an alternative method of transportation to walkers, runners, bike riders and others who shop, work and live in Alpharetta.

In its quest to provide the highest quality of life, Alpharetta is committed to a superior recreation program. Many types of programs are offered for children as well as adults. Senior citizens enjoy daily

*Equifax*

activities in a facility designed especially to meet their needs. A master plan calls for the addition of new facilities and programs each year.

Some things about Alpharetta never change, however. Each August there is an Old Soldiers Day parade down Main Street, a tradition that began right after the Civil War. During the harvest season, local farmers gather at Wills Park on Saturday mornings to sell fresh-picked fruits and vegetables. Horses graze in emerald pastures and people still wave from their front porches along the streets of Alpharetta.

The word "Alpharetta" is derived from the Greek words "Alpha" meaning first and "Retta" meaning town. It is clear the city lives up to the name as the number one place to live, work, shop and play.

*Old Soldiers Day Parade*

# FULTON COUNTY ECONOMIC DEVELOPMENT DIVISION

*I*n the fast-paced world of doing business in the 1990s, the Fulton County Economic Development Division has become a critical business relocation resource.

Created under the auspices of the Fulton County Department of Planning and Economic Development, the Economic Development Division is professionally staffed to market and promote Fulton County through comprehensive programs designed to influence commercial and industrial clients to locate and expand in Fulton County.

In Fulton County, they don't just tell you where the sources are, they actually participate with commercial lenders to help ensure that your company gets the financing it needs to grow and create jobs.

The Development Authority of Fulton County, a special-purpose Government unit, was established to make Fulton County a magnet for high-quality development activity and to assist in stimulating and diversifying the County's economy in general. The Authority's principal tool to stimulate economic development and job creation has been its power to provide low-cost debt-financing for manufacturing companies planning to expand, or construct and equip new facilities.

The Economic Development Division provides current information on local conditions, including labor, taxes, transportation and the economy. Staff members are able to help identify suitable industrial, commercial and retail business sites, as well as help solve zoning, permitting and licensing problems.

The division is made up of three unique sections: Marketing Services, Business Services and Financial Services. Each group provides a vital service to both newcomers and long-term residents in business and industry.

The Economic Development Division's Marketing Services provides timely, accurate information on potential communities, sites and available facilities to businesses in Fulton County.

Technical assistance and international market information are available through the Business Services section of the Economic Development Division. For businesses looking to compete in the global economy, the business services division can help identify and develop international markets, arrange shipping and currency exchanges, handle legal matters and prepare required documents.

The Financial Services section of the Economic Development Division provides the critical link for companies to arrange financing through commercial lenders or in-house programs. Opportunities include financing through the Economic Development Corporation of Fulton County, a certified Small Business Administration lending corporation or business improvement loans through the Community Development Block Grant.

This three-tiered approach to aggressive economic development in Fulton County adds up to a comprehensive range of services tailored to provide solutions, whether a company is just beginning to look for a new location or is a seasoned veteran with special needs.

*North Fulton construction site*

*A*s the commercial and residential real estate market has continued to boom in metro Atlanta during the last twenty years, the demand for quality residential development at every price point, and talented, aggressive agents to handle it, has escalated dramatically.

Knowledge of the market, the infrastructure and the amenities of a fast-growing community like North Fulton County are prerequisites for success in the fast-paced world of home buying and selling, and local, homegrown professionals, like J. Andy Keith and Misty M. Reid of RE/MAX Affiliates North in Roswell, have risen to the challenge.

With more than eleven years of real estate experience in North Fulton, the two Realtors™ have seen the community evolve from a quiet, rural suburb of Atlanta to a thriving, independent commercial hub with a diverse selection of housing opportunities. Between the two, they have closed over $50 million of real estate, including new homes and re-sales at every price level, from starter homes to estate homes.

As partners, J. Andy Keith and Misty M. Reid specialize in listing and selling homes throughout North Fulton. Both are native Atlantans with valuable insights into the unique facets of living in North Fulton, a tranquil, suburban setting with easy access to the thriving business hub of Atlanta.

They have a clear understanding of the diversity of the housing market in North Fulton, which offers contemporary or traditional homes, condominiums, homes with extensive property or small, cluster homes ideal for carefree lifestyles. As the area has grown in recent years, executives facing corporate relocations have come to rely on their expertise to make smooth transitions and establish roots in the south.

As RE/MAX agents, J. Andy Keith and Misty M. Reid market properties utilizing every resource available, including unusual personal touches and creative solutions. They operate under the premise that every home buyer and seller is deserving of the same level of service.

Looking forward to the next century in an area that will meet the challenge of hosting national and international sporting events like the Olympics, J. Andy Keith and Misty M. Reid are two dedicated professionals who will provide solutions and quality customer service in the competitive market of residential real estate. As North Fulton continues to grow, attracting families from all over the nation, these two leaders of RE/MAX Affiliates North will set the pace for buying and selling homes.

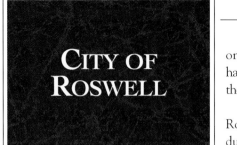

# CITY OF ROSWELL

The city of Roswell sits along the northern banks of the Chattahoochee River in North Fulton County like a jewel in the crown of metropolitan Atlanta. Twenty-five miles from midtown Atlanta, Roswell has become a prestigious address for both business and individuals.

In recent years, Roswell has obtained national recognition in the book *Fifty Fabulous Places to Raise Your Family*, and was highlighted on the Oprah Winfrey show as one of the best communities in the U.S. to live. The *Wall Street Journal* referred to Roswell as the number one "Boom Town" in the U.S. with the fastest growth from small business establishments.

Even though Roswell is now the sixth-largest city in the state, with a population of over 50,000, the community jealously guards the small-town feeling which has attracted upscale housing developments and young families. Proud of its history and vigilant to protect it, city officials designated a historic district which loosely defines the old mill town that Roswell King founded in 1839. Roswell has numerous historical sites listed on the National Register of Historic Places. Many of the pre-1900 structures not only survived the war, but have been renovated to reveal their former grandeur.

One town landmark, the Roswell Mill, was destroyed during the Civil War, later rebuilt and continued in operation until the early 1970s. It has now been renovated and features restaurants, galleries, and specialty shops as well as functioning as a town gathering spot for festivals and concerts at the amphitheater.

Roswell's award-winning recreation and parks system offers families an almost unlimited menu of outdoor and indoor recreation. The new municipal complex contains a government building, library, police facility and an auditorium with a 600-seat theater, which is home to a resident professional theater and many concerts and special events. An outstanding volunteer fire department affords the city's residents one of the highest ratings given by the insurance industry.

In addition to Fulton County schools which serve the city, there are many private elementary and high schools, kindergartens and day-care centers. Education is a top priority for the community, as evidenced by the test scores of Roswell students, which are consistently among the highest in the state.

For both businesses and individuals, Roswell represents prosperity. The 1990 census shows Roswell's average household income as $72,000, one of the highest in the United States. Among the 6,000 businesses in Roswell's economic development districts are bio-tech, medical, computer software and specialized industrial research facilities including Kimberly-Clark's research campus, AMI and North Fulton Regional Hospital.

For the last 28 years, Roswell's city government has been directed by Mayor W.L. "Pug" Mabry, with the assistance of an elected council, and an appointed city administrator.

"Because we listen to and focus great attention on families, their economic future and their needs, we have been able to create a favorable climate for future residential and business investment and prosperity for the city as a whole," said Mayor Mabry.

*Mayor W.L. "Pug" Mabry*

# FIRST COLONY BANK

At First Colony Bank, trained professionals provide a full range of products and services to individuals and businesses in the North Fulton community, skillfully combining the advantages of a large commercial financial institution with the personal service of a hometown bank.

A locally owned and operated financial institution, First Colony was chartered in July 1984 and is the oldest independent community bank in North Fulton. The operation was started with a $2.5 million capital base and over the last decade has grown to $50 million in assets. This state-chartered commercial bank is controlled by a board of directors, comprised exclusively of local businessmen, and facilitated by a twenty-member advisory board.

As a community bank, First Colony relies on a superior level of personal service to attract and constantly satisfy customers. The twenty-six-person staff is reliable, friendly, knowledgeable, and easily accessible; the checking account prices are simple; the teller service is fast; and offices are conveniently located. Standard banking operations, as well as small business and personal loan services, are available at the main office in Alpharetta and at a branch location in Roswell, which opened in 1987. Extended drive-in hours are offered at both facilities for customer convenience.

As a leading community bank, First Colony provides a full range of services to North Fulton residents, including permanent mortgage loans and Visa and MasterCards. Responsiveness, a leading edge community banks have over regional institutions, guarantee a timely decision-making process for personal and business loan applicants, and revision of major bank policies. First Colony believes in hands on management and is willing to provide the personal touch that makes community banking unique.

In addition to an inherent understanding of the community, First Colony promotes local economic development by encouraging growth of small businesses and supporting community organizations. Bank management has formed a long-term commitment with the 300 First Colony shareholders as well as the North Fulton community at large, and is committed to controlled expansion of assets and services long into the future.

As the North Fulton County economic boom continues into the next century, business leaders like First Colony Bank will provide the stability, service, and strategic vision which guarantees success.

# REINHARDT COLLEGE, THE NORTH FULTON CENTER

*A* new dimension in higher education has been brought to North Fulton through the branch program developed by Reinhardt College, one of Georgia's leading independent centers of learning.

Reinhardt is a co-educational college founded in Waleska, Georgia in 1883, which has developed a reputation for providing a quality education in an

intentionally caring environment. It is affiliated with the United Methodist Church and is accredited by the Southern Association of Colleges and Schools. Classes are offered at the main campus in Waleska, and at branch centers in North Fulton and Chatsworth.

Reinhardt's North Fulton center began offering college-level evening classes to the residents of Roswell, Alpharetta and the surrounding community during the fall of 1987. Year-round classes are held in the Education building of the Northbrook United Methodist Church in Roswell.

The curriculum of the North Fulton Center is firmly grounded in the liberal arts, and rooted in the educational premise that diversified knowledge builds basic skills and develops creative thought.

The program appeals to students of all ages who are seeking a challenging environment to establish or enhance their skills, and a convenient location. Students can pursue an associate degree in arts, business administration, pre-education or criminal justice.

Students can also take courses required by the McCamish School of Business at Reinhardt which offers a four-year degree in business, or take courses that are required by the pre-nursing degree and be admitted to area schools of nursing.

The small class size, caring faculty, opportunity for one-on-one counseling and quick, convenient registration process set Reinhardt's North Fulton location apart from other colleges. The program emphasizes effective study skills, individual attention, and a goal-oriented staff and student body. Most students are returning to the classroom as a stepping stone to increase their marketability on the job, to prepare for a career change or for general self-improvement.

The majority of the instructors at the North Fulton Center are full-time faculty from Reinhardt's main campus and classes are designed to transfer easily. All students have access to the main campus facilities including the library, financial aid, counseling and student development.

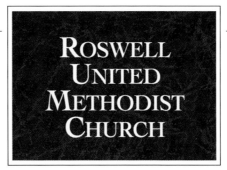

# ROSWELL UNITED METHODIST CHURCH

The tradition of caring for people and meeting their needs has been the hallmark of the Roswell United Methodist Church, establishing it as a church of vision in the North Fulton community throughout a long and rich history of progressive growth and development.

Established in 1836 as the Mount Carmel Methodist Church in a log cabin on the outskirts of the tiny mill town of Roswell, the church has kept pace with the rapid development of the area, constantly working to meet the challenges of a diverse population and their changing needs.

Since its formation, Roswell United Methodist Church has exemplified the motto, "We Care." Programs and religious services on the 15-acre campus minister to a diverse population, incorporating the traditions of the church while aggressively embracing change.

Under the direction of senior pastor Dr. Malone Dodson, the dynamic leader appointed in 1977, the church has grown from an enrollment of 432 in 1956 to more than 6,600 in 1994, and has been recognized as one of the ten fastest-growing United Methodist churches in the nation. Surrounded by the historic buildings that line Mimosa Boulevard in Roswell, the complex has expanded to five buildings, including a 700-seat chapel, sprawling educational complex, youth building, counseling center and 2,200-seat sanctuary, which was completed in 1988.

The vast size of the congregation does not prevent the direct bond of each member with the church, however. Neighborhood care groups, visitation programs, ministries that deliver tapes to shut-ins and a 24-hour prayer line put fellowship on a more personal level.

Roswell United Methodist Church has also become a vital facet of the North Fulton community at large. The full-service professionally staffed counseling center provides individual, group and family counseling as well as lectures, seminars and workshops on substance abuse, separation and divorce, vocations and stress management. Other programs,

like Seniors Enriched Living, Habitat for Humanity, and North Fulton Drug-Free, were established at Roswell United Methodist and now attract hundreds of participants.

The music ministry, directed by Dr. Michael O'Neal, attracts more than 20,000 people each year to the "Sounds of the Spirit" concert series. Performances by the 200-voice sanctuary choir and resident performing ensemble vary from traditional religious selections to a patriotic concert that has become a local summer tradition.

Concerned members of the congregation have established a highly effective singles and stepfamily

program, and one of the first Noah's Ark programs for the developmentally disabled. The youth fellowship programs include mission work locally and around the nation, involving hands-on work with the elderly and people directly in crisis.

As the church prepares to minister into the next century, focus groups are examining the needs and interests of the diverse congregation that makes Roswell United Methodist Church unique, and recharging the "inclusiveness" approach that has been the impetus for growth over the last decade.

# HISTORIC ROSWELL CONVENTION & VISITORS BUREAU

The Roswell Historic District is filled with antebellum homes and sites that survived the Civil War. Truly "The Real Old South," the District reflects the lifestyles of a wide range of society during the 1800s. Bulloch Hall (built in 1839) is the childhood home of President Theodore Roosevelt's mother, Mittie Bulloch. The 1845 Archibald Smith Plantation Home is fully furnished in period pieces, reflecting the life of a well-to-do farm family in Georgia. Roswell Presbyterian Church, used as a hospital during the War Between the States, still carries an outline of a checker-board carved on a cabinet door by convalescing soldiers. The Mill Village, mill sites, and the 1882 cotton mill are still vital to the Historic District.

Reminders of the past are numerous and, in an attempt to preserve them for future generations, the Historic Roswell District Owners & Business Association encourages their revitalization and use. Perhaps one of the best examples of an adaptive-use facility is the Roswell Founders Club located in the "Old Bricks." Built in 1840 as residence for the Roswell Mill workers, the Bricks are among the oldest apartments in the United States. The Roswell Founders Club was established in the tradition of Membership by Invitation, the signature of a fine private club. It offers members and guests an intimate environment conducive to both business and social entertaining, combining the region's finest cuisine and superb service with the warmth and charm of an elegant but comfortable antebellum residence. The Grand Ball Room, numerous private meeting rooms, and elegant dining rooms offer the perfect setting for any event, while maintaining the standards and charm of a bygone era.

Antique shops, fine art galleries, unique boutiques, restaurants, and one-of-a-kind stores housed in period storefronts fill the area.

Experience true Southern hospitality in Historic Roswell. For tours or information contact the Historic Roswell Convention & Visitors Bureau, 617 Atlanta Street, Roswell, GA 30075, or call 404-640-3253.

*A*ttention to quality and luxurious amenities are a few of the hallmarks of Huntcliff Summit, a senior adult residential community in the heart of North Fulton.

Conveniently located between historic Roswell and Sandy Springs, the

community is situated on fourteen meticulously landscaped acres of gardens, walking trails, and natural forestland.

Huntcliff Summit is one of four senior adult properties owned and managed by Laing Properties, Inc., an international real estate development, management, and investment company which was founded in England in 1848. U. S. operations for Laing, which were established in 1976, are headquartered in Atlanta and include not only senior housing, but a multitude of office buildings, business parks, and apartments.

At Huntcliff Summit, residents can select from seven premier one- and two-bedroom apartment designs, all of which offer fully equipped all-electric kitchens, private balconies, abundant storage space, and an individual emergency call system which is monitored twenty-four hours a day.

These elegant accommodations are enhanced by an array of personal services including housekeeping and linen service, on-site personal care services, and local transportation. An indoor heated pool and Jacuzzi, outdoor picnic area, and putting green are available for recreational use by all residents, who can also enjoy ongoing special events planned by the full-time Resident Services Coordinator. A beauty salon, sundry/snack shop, and complete banking services are also conveniently located on the premises.

Huntcliff Summit's Assisted Living Wing provides the added benefits and services of on-call trained staff members in the same elegant environment, including three meals per day, supervision in areas of nutrition, medications, personal hygiene, and coordination of activities and transportation.

At Huntcliff Summit, the Laing tradition of quality has created a standard of excellence for retirement living, fostering a comfortable community where residents can enjoy a gracious, affordable lifestyle.

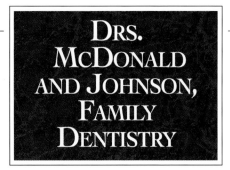

# DRS. McDONALD AND JOHNSON, FAMILY DENTISTRY

With a commitment to professional finesse, Drs. Roy McDonald and Brian Johnson have introduced dentistry with a difference to the community of North Fulton, subtly blending personal attention and state-of-the-art technology to offer full-service, contemporary dental care.

The friendly environment and well-trained staff of professionals at their Roswell office put patients of all ages immediately at ease. The doctors are committed to creating a positive experience during each visit, and encouraging good communication between the patient and their caregiver.

Dr. McDonald is a native Georgian and graduate of Emory University Dental School, who has practiced in the North Fulton area since 1983. Dr. Johnson received his D.M.D. from the Medical College of Georgia. Both dentists are members of the Academy of General Dentistry, an organization dedicated to quality in dentistry through continuing education, as well as the American Dental Association, the Georgia Dental Association, the North Fulton Dental Implant Study Club, the Academy for Implants and Transplants and several local business organizations.

In addition to routine dental care for children and adults, specialized treatments like dental surgery, including implants and cosmetic surgery, veneering, bonding and bleaching, are all available under the direction of Drs. McDonald and Johnson.

Dr. Brian Johnson

A more beautiful smile is the goal of several cosmetic procedures available with Drs. McDonald and Johnson. Reconstructive dentistry, including dental implants, which can be used to replace one tooth or an entire arch, can be done in the office. As an alternative to removable partials or dentures, implants are effective, natural-looking replacements for missing teeth. Cosmetic veneering and bonding, which is also done on-site, can change the shape and color of a smile, as well as restore decayed teeth to their natural beauty.

With an eye to the future, Drs. McDonald and Johnson have rapidly expanded their practice to incorporate the latest dental technology and welcome other professionals in their field. Their highly trained and experienced staff includes two general practitioners, an oral surgeon, a periodontist, an orthodontist and dental hygienist. Through this well-rounded staff, all of the patient's needs can be met under the direction of Drs. McDonald and Johnson and under one roof.

Dr. Roy McDonald

This attention to state-of-the-art technology is carried into all levels of patient services including sterilization techniques and account management. Drs. McDonald and Johnson's laboratory and office use the most advanced sterilization techniques available, and are monitored weekly by the Emory University Bacteriology Laboratory. Staff routinely follow all Centers for Disease Control and American Dental Association infection control guidelines. Insurance and patient billing are handled directly through a computer to ease patient's handling of accounts.

As a well-established full-service family practice, Drs. McDonald and Johnson have grown with the community by offering the most up-to-date, high-quality dentistry in a friendly, caring environment. They provide the "Gentle Dental Care" that makes each visit a positive experience for the whole family.

# NORTH FULTON REGIONAL HOSPITAL

When North Fulton Regional Hospital opened its doors to the community in 1983, the hospital filled a void that had become increasingly evident as North Fulton County launched into an explosion of growth that continues today. Constructed on a 47-acre campus strategically located between Roswell and Alpharetta on Highway 9, North Fulton Regional Hospital quickly became an essential part of the community and gained a reputation for quality healthcare services.

As the community has grown, so has North Fulton Regional Hospital. Today's modern hospital is a major contributor to the area's economy and has invested $75 million over the past decade.

With a staff of more than 900 health-care professionals, the hospital is among the largest employ-

ers in the North Fulton area. Approximately 400 physicians are on the hospital's medical staff. In addition, some 325 community residents volunteer their time and talents to the hospital on a regular basis.

Licensed for 167 beds, North Fulton Regional

Hospital is one of the few hospitals in the Atlanta area to offer all private rooms to patients. Even though NFRH has managed to maintain the comfortable atmosphere of a community hospital, it has steadily expanded and now offers a wide range of services and technologically advanced equipment usually found only in much larger facilities.

NFRH's 12,000-square-foot emergency department—with separate patient rooms including separate cardiac, trauma and orthopaedic areas—is one of the finest in metro Atlanta. The area is staffed with full-time board-certified emergency medicine physicians and other personnel specially trained in emergency medicine.

The hospital is also a state-designated Level II adult trauma center, one of only three in the greater Atlanta area. To be so designated, the hospital must meet a wide range of criteria, including 24-hour operating room, surgical subspecialities immediately available and in-house anesthesia.

The hospital's Women's Heath Center has grown in recent years to become the facility of choice for an increasing number of women giving birth. With modern, private labor-delivery-recovery rooms, giving birth is truly a family experience. And if needed, the hospital also has a neonatal intensive care unit staffed round-the-clock with a neonatologist, specially trained nurses and a respiratory therapist.

In line with a growing national trend, NFRH established within the hospital an outpatient surgery unit with its own separate entrance. The unit has centralized admission and discharge to save patient's time and stress. Patients taking advantage of the outpatient surgery unit have access to the same accommodations, care and state-of-the-art technology available to patients admitted to the hospital.

NFRH also operates its own pain control center, provides both inpatient and outpatient rehabilitation, lithotripsy, ultrasound, nuclear cardiology and diagnostic services such as computerized tomography (CT) and magnetic resonance imaging (MRI).

The hospital recognizes the role it plays in promoting the general wellness of the residents of the community it serves. In this regard, North Fulton Regional Hospital offers hundreds of classes and seminars—many of them at no charge—on a variety of subjects appropriate for children and adults. In addition, the hospital also offers a free physician referral service to newcomers to the area or to others who wish to locate a physician in a particular specialty.

As the hospital enters its second decade of service to the community, it will continue to grow with the area. NFRH reaffirms its commitment to quality health care and to be the preferred hospital for the residents of North Fulton county.

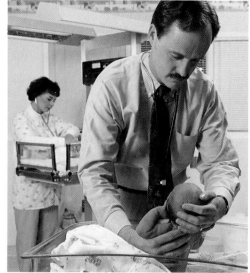

© Stan Kaady

Photo Courtesy of North Fulton Regional Hospital

# SAINT JOSEPH'S HOSPITAL OF ATLANTA

Saint Joseph's Hospital of Atlanta, one of the finest medical institutions in the Southeast, is a hospital rich in tradition, rich in technical excellence and rich in personal care. Hundreds of North Fulton residents benefit each year from the medical services provided by Atlanta's oldest hospital, founded by the Sisters of Mercy.

Since it was established as a premier health-care facility, Saint Joseph's has attracted some of the nation's best physicians. Patients come from all over the Southeast and other parts of the country because of the facility's reputation for dignified care.

Saint Joseph's history dates back to 1831 when Catherine McAuley founded the Sisters of Mercy in Dublin, Ireland to help serve the poor. In 1880, Sister Cecilia Carroll and three companions traveled from Savannah, Georgia to minister to the sick and open the first medical facility in Atlanta — known today as Saint Joseph's Hospital.

As a 346-bed acute-care, specialty-referral hospital, Saint Joseph's is highly respected for its cardiology, vascular, oncology, orthopaedic and gastroin-testinal programs, as well as for numerous other specialties.

Saint Joseph's performed the first open-heart surgery and angioplasty procedures in the Southeast and opened the region's first cardiac catheterization lab and pacemaker clinic. The hospital's Heart Institute performs more open-heart surgeries and cardiac catheterizations than any other facility in the Southeast and operates one of the most extensive heart transplant programs in the country.

Saint Joseph's is also one of a few select hospitals nationwide designated by the National Cancer Institute as a Community Clinical Oncology Program. This designation gives Saint Joseph's the ability to perform cancer treatments not available outside major research settings.

The Orthopaedic Services program at Saint Joseph's offers a full range of services. Severe fractures, prolonged pain, arthritic complications, athletic and work-related injuries and deteriorating diseases are just some of the problems treated at the hospital.

Regarded as one of Georgia's early pioneers in vascular surgery, Saint Joseph's provides a wide-variety of diagnostic and treatment capabilities for diseases that prevent the normal flow of blood in veins and arteries. Moreover, the hospital's expanded Gastrointestinal Diagnostic Unit successfully treats a multitude of digestive system disorders.

Saint Joseph's top priority is teaming skilled physicians with experienced nurses and other medical personnel. This dedication to a team approach ensures the best plan of treatment for North Fulton patients.

Beyond Saint Joseph's deep commitment to heal the whole patient lies a responsibility to help the poor, the homeless and those less fortunate. In 1993 alone, Saint Joseph's and its parent company, Saint Joseph's Health System, contributed almost $21 million in charity care and community outreach. Principles of stewardship and collaboration with other North Fulton health-care providers are of utmost importance for the community's continued growth and prosperity.

Photo Courtesy of Saint Joseph's Hospital of Atlanta

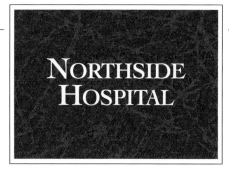

# NORTHSIDE HOSPITAL

$\mathcal{N}$orthside Hospital is one of Atlanta's leading full-service, not-for-profit health-care institutions, earning a regional reputation through its offerings in Women's Services, Oncology, Emergency Services, Behavioral Services and Surgery. This 455-bed hospital cares for more than 100,000 patients annually.

Northside Hospital ranks as one of the country's top hospitals for newborn deliveries (almost 8,500 deliveries annually), insuring both mother and baby the broadest range of care and expertise. The hospital offers a Perinatal Diagnostic Center for high-risk pregnancies, a Lactation Center for breast-feeding education, and a Mother-Baby unit to link the mother and the baby with the same nurse.

Northside Hospital's excellence continues beyond women's care, however. The hospital is also home to the Institute for Cancer Control, a regional oncology center providing prevention, detection, treatment, research, rehabilitation and support services to cancer patients. The hospital also offers ScreenAtlanta[sm], a program that provides low-cost health screenings and educational services through a mobile unit.

The Emergency Services department at Northside Hospital provides vital emergency care to more than 30,000 patients annually, and further proves its commitment to the health of the community through Health Express, a minor injury and illness center that offers quick and efficient treatment.

*Northside Hospital/Alpharetta*

Northside Hospital serves the behavioral needs of North Fulton through mental health and substance abuse programs, in addition to a Sleep Disorders Center. The Sleep Disorders Center is the first of its kind accredited in Georgia, and uses the latest technology to treat conditions such as snoring, sleep apnea and insomnia.

Reminiscent of the growth that led to the creation of Northside Hospital in 1970, rapid development in the Alpharetta area prompted a land purchase near State Bridge Road and Georgia Highway 400. The hospital currently offers an outpatient cancer treatment center, an outpatient surgery center, community education programs and a medical office building on the Northside Hospital/Alpharetta campus.

Northside Hospital is proud of its service within the convenience and comfort of a neighborhood setting, and looks forward to its continued and shared growth with the North Fulton community.

*A*re children really so special that they need their own hospital? Scottish Rite Children's Medical Center first answered "yes" to that question in 1915, and the families of Atlanta, Georgia, and the region have gratefully agreed ever since.

Scottish Rite was originally founded in Decatur, Georgia, as a charity facility to address the unmet needs of poor children with orthopaedic disabilities. A fortunate combination of community support and medical expertise helped the new hospital grow, soon bringing it national recognition for the care it provided its young patients. In 1976, the hospital moved to its present campus in North Fulton and began to serve more and more of the medical needs of children.

The scope of Scottish Rite's current facilities and technological capabilities would certainly amaze the civic leaders from whose vision they grew. But those civic leaders would no doubt recognize the same loving dedication to children and families that has been the hallmark of Scottish Rite since its inception.

Today, Scottish Rite meets the unique medical needs of children and adolescents through forty medical subspecialties. It offers a 24-hour pediatric emergency/trauma center staffed with private-practice, board-certified and board-eligible pediatricians. Many of the pediatric specialty programs affiliated with the Medical Center serve families from throughout the Southeast. It even has a phone line (250-KIDS) for concerned parents to speak with a Scottish Rite nurse, seven days a week between 4 PM and 6 AM when the pediatrician's office may be closed.

Scottish Rite is located on 18-1/2 acres near the junction of I 285 and Georgia Highway 400. Its campus includes facilities for the 165-bed Wilbur and Hilda Glenn Hospital for Children and the Children's Medical Center Professional Building. From this "home base" in North Fulton, Scottish Rite has responded to the needs of surrounding areas, establishing specialty-care facilities in Cobb and Gwinnett counties and in the Southern Crescent region. Private-practice emergency physicians from the Scottish Rite Medical Staff also serve the pediatric emergency centers at Cobb Hospital and Medical Center and Gwinnett Medical Center.

Yes, children and adolescents really are special, and Scottish Rite has made service and quality cornerstones of its mission of serving them. Committed to providing excellent pediatric care at an appreciable value and in a nurturing environment, Scottish Rite cares for kids from A to Z.

© Stan Kaddy

80

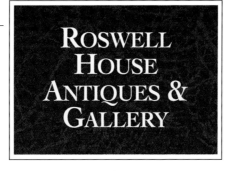

# ROSWELL HOUSE ANTIQUES & GALLERY

A flair for international art and fine European antiques has been brought to Roswell's historic district by Fausto and Marcia Gardini, recent new owners of the Roswell House Antiques & Gallery on Canton Street.

After first visiting Georgia in 1976 from his homeland, the Grand-Duchy of Luxembourg, Fausto Gardini was attracted to the Atlanta area and moved here from Europe in 1984. Avid collectors of fine 19th-century art, Fausto and Marcia Gardini established a showcase for their treasures in a quaint former residence in Roswell. The meticulous restoration of the interior of the 54-year-old former private home in the shopping district adjacent to the historic town square set the stage for the exhibition of the many artifacts assembled.

Marcia and Fausto's art collection includes paintings by renowned British artists like James Clark Sr., A. Jackson and Charles Foot Tayler. French 19th-century artists represented are, among others, Francois Emile de Lansac, Eugene Leliepvre and André LeGuay.

A select collection of first edition and/or autographed books, with a special emphasis on Southern authors, is also part of the vast inventory, a treasure-trove for the discerning collector. Authors represented include Truman Capote, Olive Ann Burns, Anne Edwards, Betsy Fancher, James Grady, Paul Hemphill, Margaret Mitchell, Robert M. Myers, Eugenia Price, Alexandra Ripley, Celestine Sibley, Anne Rivers Siddons, W.B. Williford and many more.

The Roswell House Antiques & Gallery displays, in the 'Rare Books and Manuscripts Gallery' of the recently opened 'Road to Tara Museum' in Atlanta, an important collection of Margaret Mitchell's epic novel *Gone With the Wind*. The collection consists of 15 different American and some 20 foreign editions of the enduring publication. The Roswell House Antiques & Gallery also proudly owns several rare school books of the beloved author.

Special events hosted at the Roswell House Antiques & Gallery aim at stimulating the interest of local residents in European culture, as well as attracting dignitaries and foreign representatives to Roswell. Honored guests at the inauguration of the exhibition, "Luxembourg On My Mind," hosted there in late 1993, were H.E. Alphonse Berns, Ambassador of the Grand-Duchy of Luxembourg to the United States as well as Robert Schaeffer, Consul General with residence in Kansas City, Missouri. The week-long exhibition showcased this beautiful little country, a determined and faithful ally of the United States. A recent effort started in Luxembourg as "Hands Across the Atlantic–The Luxembourg Relief Fund," allowed the collection of a substantial sum in support to the flood victims in the Midwestern states. Fausto and Marcia Gardini look forward to continue receiving visitors, guests and friends at the Roswell House Antiques & Gallery on Canton Street.

*"Goldfinch," the oil on canvas portrait of a grey mare in a loose box by James Clark, is an example of the fine art on display at the Roswell House Antiques & Gallery. Clark was a successful itinerant animal portraitist with commissions from many well-known landed gentry, including William Ward Talby of Quemby Hall. This piece is signed and inscribed "Newmarket."*

# NORTH FULTON CIVIC ORGANIZATIONS

◆

As the community of North Fulton has expanded, numerous social service agencies and volunteer organizations have effectively met the challenge of providing a good standard of living for all residents, regardless of income.

For generations, volunteers have united with churches, businesses and civic groups to provide creative solutions to North Fulton families in need. And the solutions go far beyond adequate food, clothing, shelter and medical care.

In North Fulton, county-based agencies and local chapters of national volunteer organizations address the growing need for affordable child care, employment alternatives for the mentally handicapped and lifestyle enrichment programs for the elderly. Every day, people are reaching out to help others.

From the teachers at the North Fulton Child Development Center to the workers putting the finishing touches on homes for Habitat for Humanity, there is a universal commitment to caring for other members of the community and providing a certain quality of life.

This type of community support was inherent to the founding of the North Fulton Child Development Center and is still an intricate part of the organization's success. Established through the efforts of local churches, the center provides an affordable alternative for quality pre-school child care to low-income families.

Community leaders began researching the project in 1967 and organized a makeshift facility in a local church until a permanent site was established on Grove Way in Roswell. Through the generous support of several North Fulton community groups and the efforts of dedicated volunteers, the building was eventually purchased and renovated into a multi-purpose facility in 1976.

As a state-licensed facility, the center provides a welcome alternative to parents who might otherwise have to face the risks of unsupervised caregivers. More than 100 children, aged three months through six years, attend the center daily.

In addition to the full-time teaching staff, the children in the center benefit from the expertise of a speech therapist, recreational therapist, educational consultant and social worker.

Many local businesses provide equipment and supplies, as well as sponsor scholarships, for needy families, and also subsidize essential expenses, such as a medical fund. Over the years the North Fulton Child Development Center has also developed programs to meet the special needs of the parents, such as a weekly support group that offers presentations on parenting skills and other relevant issues.

The center is also supported by volunteers from the Chattahoochee Cotillion Club, a nonprofit

*Georgia Festival, Sandy Springs*

*Roswell Arts Festival*

organization of young women from North Fulton who work in the community throughout the year prior to making their debut at Bulloch Hall. Representatives of the 40-member group are shaking off their "white glove" image and channeling their social energy into local projects through both financial assistance and direct, hands-on volunteer hours.

The North Fulton Human Resource Center, the permanent site of the North Fulton Community Charities and a temporary center for the Roswell branch of the North Fulton Senior Services, was established in 1983 as a cooperative venture by area churches, businesses and service groups. Through donations and with the help of volunteers, the Center operates a clothes closet, food pantry, and provides emergency financial assistance to North Fulton families.

The Clothes Closet is a thrift store for household items, clothing and furniture. Although items are unit-priced to the general public, arrangements are made to give essentials to people with extraordinary needs at no charge. The Food Pantry provides those same families with food staples and non-perishable items during the critical transition period before county assistance is in place.

The emergency shelter division of the North Fulton Human Resource Center became a separate nonprofit corporation, Housing Initiative in North Fulton Inc., in 1993. The organization started with three homes donated by the U.S. Department of Housing and Urban Development which were renovated for use as temporary family crisis centers.

Housing Initiative assists North Fulton residents in need of safe, affordable housing as well as providing transitional shelter through the "Homestretch" program. The project is staffed by volunteers from local churches and funded by private donations and corporate contributions.

Another aspect of the multi-service Human Resource Center is providing meals and recreational activities to North Fulton senior citizens. It is currently one of two county-operated senior centers north of the Chattahoochee River.

North Fulton Senior Services, the county-based management arm for the centers, is one of three nonprofit agencies established in 1991 in Fulton County and functions under the umbrella of the Atlanta Regional Commission. The three-tiered organization replaced the now-defunct Senior Services of Metro Atlanta. Two other operations providing similar services operate in the central and south zones of Fulton County. Each agency has a separate board of directors to oversee operations and establish policies.

The mission of the North Fulton agency is to provide for the well, but frail, elderly members of the community. Senior centers are currently located in Roswell and Alpharetta with plans for additional facilities to come on-line in the near future. Planned activities and hot, nutritional meals are provided in the centers, which also function as the preparation sites for more than 100 home meals delivered throughout the area.

When the agency was established there were very limited transportation services and only 29 home-delivered meals to seniors. As the needs of the over-60 population have increased, the Roswell senior center has been completely refurbished, the Alpharetta facility has opened and transportation now reaches 95 percent of the clients using the centers.

Managers at each center coordinate activities and programs with the help of a Site Council, a core group of senior volunteers. Community members are often invited to present programs on a

# Emily Dolvin

Behind the soft-spoken genteel Southern Lady is the steel spirit that has carried Emily Gordy Dolvin — "Sissy" to her friends — from the community groups of Roswell to the family chambers at the White House.

Out of her turn-of-the-century Victorian cottage nestled in the shadow of stately Bulloch Hall in Roswell's Historic District, Mrs. Dolvin has orchestrated the formation and development of countless organizations that have created a comfortable quality of life in North Fulton's largest city.

The petite but powerful woman has left a distinctive mark on the organizations that make Roswell tick, from the Historical Society to the Recreation Association to the North Fulton Community Charities.

As newlyweds and newcomers to the tiny, rural community in 1938, Mrs. Dolvin and her husband William Jasper played an active role in all aspects of Roswell living. Mr. Dolvin, whose impact on education is recognized by the Alpharetta elementary school named in his honor, served as principal of Roswell Elementary School and president of the teacher's association for more than a decade.

Mrs. Dolvin was instrumental in the formation of the city recreation department, raising funds to build the first municipal tennis courts at Waller Park, and went on to serve as a commissioner in the Recreation Association for ten years. She was also a charter member of the Roswell Historical Society and served as the organization's third president.

During her period of community leadership in Roswell, Mrs. Dolvin was also a highly visible player in the state political arena, often at the side of her nephew, former President Jimmy Carter.

Acting on suggestions by Mrs. Dolvin, who was affectionately called the "little colonel," the stately governor's mansion on West Paces Ferry Road in Atlanta was opened to the public for the first time during Mr. Carter's tenure as governor. The hostess program and information about the building still in circulation were created under Mrs. Dolvin's critical eye.

The Roswell matron was also an important figure in Jimmy Carter's 1976 presidential campaign, visiting 40 of the nation's 50 states, and was a proud face in the crowd at the inauguration of America's 38th president.

variety of topics including crafts, gardening, painting, income tax or healthcare forms.

Intergenerational programs are also well received by both the clients at the senior centers and North Fulton students. In recent years, Alpharetta seniors have been pen pals with second-grade students, provided essential information for oral histories compiled by middle-school students and facilitated a video produced by students from Milton High School.

Volunteers are a vital link in the success of the programs and are the sole means of meal delivery in North Fulton. More than 250 people from civic and religious groups like the Windward Association of Retired Men and St. Anne's Church service the regular weekly delivery routes.

Community support, specifically from area businesses, has also helped build the supply network reaching senior citizens. In addition to offering discounts and special promotions, local food retailers, like Kroger and Harry's Farmers Market, supply day-old bakery items and produce for distribution. AT&T, a strong corporate presence in Alpharetta, has made contributions to support large capital expenditures for specialized transportation and equipment.

The administrative offices for North Fulton Senior Services and the Roswell Senior Center were recently relocated to a new site on Warsaw Road as part of the long-range plan by the Fulton County Office of Aging. A new Sandy Springs center is also part of the master plan to enhance the hot-meal delivery service which operates out of Sandy Springs United Methodist Church.

Other long-range plans for the agency include construction of a multi-purpose center in Sandy Springs. Fulton County has already allocated $1.5 million for the purchase of the property but a site has not yet been determined.

The center would function as a clearinghouse for county agencies like the Department of Family and Children Services, and provide a food bank, clothing closet and healthcare services for seniors. Although the county would continue to provide meals and programming at each of the community centers, the multi-purpose facility would have

*Bellringers at the Roswell Arts Festival*

recreational activities and services on a larger scale.

Another nonprofit organization which provides services for North Fulton seniors is Seniors Enriched Living, a group formed in 1989 to enhance the quality of life for the area's retired community. One of the group's main programs is "Lunch 'n Learn," an ongoing series of quarterly classes sponsored by 15 area churches and synagogues, corporations like First Union and First Colony Bank, and civic groups like the Roswell Rotary and Lions clubs. Each week qualified volunteers present a broad variety of topics of special interest to the senior community, exploring everything from self-hypnosis to the bestsellers list. Each session attracts 250–300 participants.

In addition to the seminars, Seniors Enriched Living provides transportation to the elderly in the Roswell-Alpharetta area, acts as a referral service for medical and legal inquiries and assists with minor home repairs.

Seniors Enriched Living is modeled after Shepherd's Center of America, an organization of community-based volunteer groups represented by more than 100 facilities in 26 states, perpetuating the idea of "older adults helping older adults."

Other nonprofit organizations like Resources and Residential Alternatives, local chapters of the Georgia Federation of Women's Clubs and organizations affiliated with Rotary International work to meet the special needs of various groups in North Fulton, including the mentally and physically challenged.

Resources and Residential Alternatives was started in 1979 by a group of concerned North Fulton parents to orchestrate group homes, on-site and community employment and social activities for members of the community with special needs.

For many parents faced by the challenge of a child with mental retardation, it is like a dream come true. Since the program was established, with a group home in Roswell and Alpharetta, six more homes and two apartments in North Fulton have been added to accommodate the growing demand for residential facilities for the mentally retarded.

The homes are financed by private funds and federal grants through the Department of Housing and Urban Development. All are fully supervised by Resources and Residential Alternatives staff, who

*Georgia Youth Day Parade*

monitor daily activities and encourage independent survival skills in the 40 resident clients. Van service is provided for each home and one large transportation vehicle operates out of the administration center on Old Ellis Road in Roswell.

A support employment program and contract labor workshop was added to the services provided by Resources and Residential Alternatives in 1990, but the program is already overflowing. The workshop offers closely supervised labor-intensive jobs, like cutting and assembly work, to prepare clients to

*North Fulton Child Development Center*

work in a competitive environment where they are integrated with non-disabled peers.

Resources and Residential Alternatives works closely with North Fulton businesses. For clients ready to make the transition to community employment, opportunities have been created with leading North Fulton operations like Kroger, AT&T and Herman Miller.

Several branches of the Georgia Federation of Women's Clubs provide volunteer services and financial support to community agencies in North Fulton. The state of Georgia, which joined the federation in 1897, boasts approximately 7,000 members in 175 clubs and is headquartered in Atlanta.

In addition to servicing individual communities, the Tallulah Falls School, a boarding school for 140 students in grades 6–12, is recognized as one of the most significant contributions of the Georgia Women's Clubs. The school was built in the Georgia mountains in 1909 to provide educational opportunities to the children of the area and is still operated and supported by clubs throughout the state.

The Alpharetta Junior Women's Club supports the Tallulah Falls School as well as other community groups like Canine Companions for Independence, which provides service dogs to the physically challenged.

The Roswell Junior Women's Club, which was formed in 1980, plays a critical role in the conservation movement in North Fulton as an active participant in the "Adopt-a-Stream" program. Representatives of the 45-member service organization are also credited with landscaping the newly constructed bridge over Vickery Creek which links the trail system in the Chattahoochee National Park.

The club is the creator and sole sponsor of the Roswell Arts Festival held on the town's historic square each May. In recent years the celebration has gotten so large that future plans call for it to become part of the spring Antebellum Festival, which is held in conjunction with the annual "Colors Celebration."

Another ongoing community service program of the Roswell Junior Women's Club is to supply "care packages" of personal items to women at the rape crisis center in Grady Hospital, the only violent-crime

*Georgia Festival, Sandy Springs*

treatment center for women in Fulton County.

The Junior League of Gwinnett and North Fulton Counties, a women's service organization formed in 1986, also plays a critical role in community service operations throughout the area, placing more than 400 volunteers in county agencies each year. The organization is part of an international federation of 300 nonprofit Leagues in the United States, Canada, Great Britain and Mexico.

Two programs introduced in North Fulton by the Junior League have provided educational enrichment to school-age children. Project Self-Esteem, a classroom-based program which emphasizes self-worth through role playing, and the STAR house, an after-school enrichment program for at-risk children ages 6–12, have become valuable assets to the North Fulton community.

In Sandy Springs, 150 community leaders and local activists formed the Sandy Springs Society in 1988 to lend financial support to area charities. In the past, funds have been directed toward the restoration of the Williams-Payne house, the North Fulton Senior Services Meals on Wheels program, the Big Trees project, the Link Counseling Center and the Sandy Springs Community Action Center.

North Fulton Rotary Clubs also provide positive community outreach efforts. In addition to the annual high school leadership awards, the Roswell Rotary Club recently sponsored the "Leadership 2000 Forum," an informational, skills-building session for more than 80 carefully selected high school students.

# THE NORTH FULTON
# LIFESTYLE

◆

In the early 1970s, Bill Murtough, the executive director of the National Historic Register, swept through the South investigating historic communities. North Fulton County, with several homes dating from the 1800s in Roswell, Alpharetta and Sandy Springs, was an important stop on the tour.

Roswell city officials contacted the historical committee of the local women's club to rally support among homeowners and local residents. A separate organization grew from those early meetings and evolved into the 700-member Roswell Historical Society that is to this day responsible for preservation and restoration in the 640-acre designated historic district.

Since its formation with 172 members in 1971, the Roswell Historical Society has been committed to preserving and restoring the community's priceless link with the past.

Atlanta historian Franklin Garrett helped create the constitution and bylaws that govern the 20-year-old organization. Emily Dolvin, the society's third president, supervised the installation of historic property markers and helped design the walking tour map still in service today.

A core of community volunteers worked closely with city officials to purchase and restore Bulloch Hall, home to one of Roswell's founding families, through a bond referendum passed in 1978. Members contributed both funding and sweat equity to

*Fishing on the Chattahoochee River*

preserve the property and create a research library, furnished with period pieces, called Mittie's Room.

The cottage at Bulloch Hall served as a makeshift headquarters for the Historical Society until 1984, when attention was turned to Allenbrook, another "at risk" historic property in Roswell. Through a joint agreement by the city, the Historical Society and the National Park Service who owns the land, the former Ivy Woolen Mill superintendent's brick salt-box-style home was restored both as a welcome center for visitors and as a temporary headquarters for the Roswell Historical Society.

After several relocations, the Roswell Historical Society has found a permanent home at the Smith Plantation. The organization set up shop in one of the outbuildings on the site in January, 1992. In addition to cataloging artifacts and restoring certain areas of the property, Historical Society volunteers act as docents in period dress for ongoing tours and educational programs.

Other preservation efforts and walking tours of the entire Roswell Historic district are coordinated by the group at the new headquarters. The Historical Society is actively coordinating the third phase of an archaeological excavation of the original mill foundation built in the 1830s. They are also assisting with marking the graves in the Pleasant Hill Cemetery which date back to the 1850s.

Similar preservation efforts are underway in

Alpharetta, under the direction of the Alpharetta Historical Society. The Mansell House, a 1910 Victorian home, was recently restored and is being used as a museum and headquarters for the organization.

The home was saved from the wrecking ball by a group of city activists who purchased it from Herman Miller for the token sum of $1 and arranged for its relocation to the current site on Marietta Street in Alpharetta. The property was restored through funding from the state, the Fulton County Arts Council and private donations to the Alpharetta Historical Society.

The Mansell House reflects turn-of-the-century

*Presbyterian Church, Roswell*

middle-class life in rural Georgia. Donations by local commercial ventures like First Colony Bank helped furnish the property. A formal garden next to a trellised side entrance is also part of the master plan.

The Alpharetta Historical Society is also working to acquire and relocate the Walker home, now on Roswell Street. The pre–Civil War home of Colonel Golden Walker will be moved to property adjacent to the Mansell House and function as a reference library for the organization.

Another ongoing North Fulton preservation project has been the relocation and restoration of the historic Williams-Payne property in Sandy Springs.

The home was built by Walter Jerome Williams in 1869 on a sizable piece of farmland at the current intersection of Mount Vernon Highway and Georgia 400. In 1939, Major and Marie Payne bought the house, moved it back from the road 80 feet and completely remodeled it into a country cottage. The home remained as a residential property until 1982 when Portman-Barry Investors acquired the house and land from the Paynes for future commercial development.

In response to pleas from a grassroots community group called the "Save the Springs Movement," the investors agreed to donate the house to the Sandy Springs Garden Club in 1984. Seven members of this charter organization later formed the Sandy Springs Historic Community Foundation, with the goal of preserving the natural spring site for which the area is named and establishing a historic museum.

The group was also instrumental in persuading Fulton County to purchase 2.8 acres of land on Sandy Springs Circle, site of five freshwater springs that once served as a camping place for Indians on hunting trips and a source of water for early settlers.

The spring property was leased to the Sandy Springs Historic Community Foundation, and a new resting spot for the Williams-Payne home was selected. The building's true age was discovered during the dismantling and moving process.

A 19th-century wooden cover was used to construct a shelter over the springs, and other outbuildings were relocated to the site, including a fully

restored 1860 milk house and a late-19th-century privy. The milk house, built by James Franklin Burdett, was originally located near Mount Paran Road and Lake Forest Drive before being moved to the central historic compound.

Restoration and furnishing of the Williams-Payne house to its original 1870s appearance took almost five years. Period flooring, much of it discovered in an old mill in Lawrenceville, runs throughout the main living areas, and the four fireplaces were completely reconstructed. Furnishings and household articles which accurately portray the Reconstruction period in the South were acquired through donations and fund-raising efforts in the community. A contemporary basement with a large meeting room and office space was also added to the building.

The lavish gardens surrounding the main house and outbuildings have been completely restored and have an abundance of historically significant native plantings, including herb, meadow, bog and forest gardens.

When the $250,000 refurbishment was completed, the home opened for tours in May 1990, sparking a great deal of community interest. Since then, the Foundation has developed a special program for school children to be brought to the house on group tours. The classes are greeted by docents in period costumes, and the students see a video of the history of the community and the site, then tour the grounds and the house where many try their hand at butter churning or candle dipping.

Storytelling takes place at the Williams-Payne house on the second and fourth Saturday of each month with special guests, including leading members of the Southern Order of Storytellers, such as its founder, Carmen Agra Deedy.

The Foundation's major fund-raiser is the Sandy

Springs Festival, an arts and crafts fair held on the streets surrounding the historic site each fall. In addition to raising operating funds, the fair heightens community awareness of the historic roots of the area.

Each September, a crowd of more than 10,000 people converge on Sandy Springs Circle to visit more than 100 arts and crafts booths, run in the 5K and 10K road race, and enjoy an antique car show, a pet parade and continuous live musical entertainment.

*Evening at American Pie*

The festival, which started as a founder's day celebration, focuses on the heritage of Sandy Springs but is also designed to build community enthusiasm. Old-time crafters are on hand to demonstrate their skills in blacksmithing, quilting and lace making, and special guests have included visitors from the Cherokee Indian Reservation in North Carolina.

A second fund-raiser, introduced in 1993, is the Christmas Candlelight Tour of North Fulton's Historic Homes. Featured in the special holiday event are the Williams-Payne house, Bulloch Hall and Barrington Hall in Roswell. At each of the properties, guides in period dress recreate the typical lifestyle of the resident families during the holiday season.

Other North Fulton communities host festivals throughout the year, many of which are tied to the historic roots of the community or local arts organizations. The annual Heritage Days Celebration at Bulloch Hall is a wonderful opportunity for adults and children to take a step back in time.

Realistic demonstrations of Civil War encampments on the antebellum estate are enhanced by the ongoing demonstrations of chores from the mid-1800s like butter churning, quilting and open-hearth cooking. Storytellers and entertainers in period dress keep crowds enthralled throughout the weekend celebration with folklore, music and dance from the pre–Civil War period.

Each spring, crowds are again drawn to Roswell for the Antebellum Spring Festival. The celebration is sponsored by the Historic Roswell District Owners and Business Association and the Historic Roswell Visitors Center. Activities include ongoing tours of historic homes, entertainment by local musicians and arts and crafts booths on the town square.

The May Antebellum Festival acts as the kick-off for the summer Concerts on the Square, a series of free outdoor performances by local ensembles at the quaint gazebo and on the sprawling lawn of the Roswell town square.

The free concert series, which debuted in 1991, is sponsored by the City of Roswell and the Historic Preservation Commission. The series provides a welcome opportunity for families to enjoy a variety of musical entertainment and picnic in a casual, outdoor setting. Entertainers include country and folk musicians, the North Fulton Community Band, the Atlanta Brassworks and the Army Ground Forces Jazz Band.

The North Fulton Community Band is a 60-member orchestra formed in 1979 to fill a musical gap in North Fulton. Each year, local volunteer musicians play to increasing numbers at popular locations like the Roswell Auditorium or from center stage during the summer concert series.

The band, which is based at Roswell First United Methodist Church on historic Mimosa Boulevard, presents eight community concerts each season. Although many of the band's members are former professionals, amateur players are also welcome to participate.

In recent years the North Fulton Community Band has gained recognition outside of Atlanta by doing recordings for Kendor Music Inc., a major music publisher based in Delevan, New York. The group makes demonstration tapes of 10–12 publications

*Georgia 400 Run/Walk*

each year, which are then distributed to schools and music retailers, who order sheet music from the selections. It is the only community band to record at this level, and to date, more than 500,000 copies of the recordings done by the band are distributed throughout the United States and have been retaped in seven foreign languages.

Another tradition in community music is the Alpharetta Courthouse Singing, the oldest recognized continually-held public event in North Fulton. Singers use an early American form of six-part a cappella singing called "shape note" or "Fa So La," and the cherished tradition is now in its 125th year.

Orchestra Atlanta, a 55-member volunteer community ensemble formed in 1984, offers another dimension to the musical potential of North Fulton. The talented collection of local musicians is based at the Roswell Municipal Auditorium, the new, acoustically superior 600-seat facility in Roswell.

Formerly the Sandy Springs Chamber Orchestra,

*Ballet Class*

the group was established by Sandy Springs violin player Tom Hallam, who had a vision of bringing a community orchestra with talented musicians to north Atlanta. A chamber orchestra contains the same instrumental sections as a symphony orchestra—specifically strings, woodwind, brass and percussion, but on a smaller scale.

Under the artistic direction of conductor Philip Rice, the group performs classical medleys of famous composers like Bach, Handel, Haydn, Mozart, Beethoven and Schubert. In addition to the traditional five-concert season at the Roswell auditorium, Orchestra Atlanta performs at local fund-raisers and provides quartets or trios for special events by area organizations like the Greater North Fulton Chamber of Commerce and the AT&T Challenge. Guest performers are often invited to appear with the ensemble during the regular season, drawing even more interest and enthusiasm from North Fulton audiences.

Nationally acclaimed artists that have performed with the Orchestra in the past include concert violinist Sidney Harth, pianist Lee Luvisi, cellist Leslie Parnas and Julius Baker, former principal flutist of the New York Philharmonic.

In addition to these local musical ensembles, Northside music lovers can enjoy big-name, outdoor entertainment at the Roswell Mill Concert Series which runs from early June through the fall each year. The Rock 'n Roll Oldies series features top-name entertainers like Paul Revere & The Raiders, The Shirelles, Chubby Checker and Gary Puckett.

Concert goers can choose from individual tickets, tables, series tickets or deluxe seating on the balcony overlooking the stage. The summer concert series has helped the Roswell Mill become a vibrant focal point in the heart of Roswell's historic district. The glossy heart-pine floors, trendy restaurants and upscale boutiques high above Vickery Creek are attracting ever-increasing crowds of diners, shoppers and concert goers to the Mill each summer.

Mimms Enterprises, one of Atlanta's premier commercial redevelopers, has been the key ingredient in the Mill's resurgence as a recreation complex. When the Roswell Manufacturing Company

*Rowing on the Chattahoochee River*

vacated the building in 1975, the property fell into disrepair until it was purchased in 1984 by developer Gary Keel. A marginal restoration effort was made and the complex reopened as a specialty shopping center. The venture was not successful and the mill changed hands again in 1991, when Mimms purchased the property. Mimms immediately addressed the critical issue of visibility for the complex by purchasing land on Highway 120 and the Roswell Square and gaining the street exposure critical to success. For the first time, the developer and the city united forces to make the Mill successful as a convention-style entertainment facility, rezoning for additional signage and access from Highway 120.

The culmination of this community support was the grand reopening of the fully renovated Mill complex in April 1992. Now, whether for dining, dancing or an evening under the stars, the Mill is an ideal venue for North Fulton residents.

The three original buildings built in 1882 are part of a large entertainment complex which includes a special events facility, a large deck for outdoor concerts, and a 45,000-square-foot restaurant and retail complex. Downstairs is a model railroad depicting Roswell in the mid-1800s, lively entertainment, and scrumptious smells emanating from the restaurants and piano bars.

Diners enjoy the historic setting of the Roswell Mill and the variety of restaurant choices, from Mexican or German cuisine to gourmet Continental fare. Traditional Atlanta dining spots like Aunt Fanny's Cabin have set up facilities at the Mill, which draws visitors from all parts of the city.

Several other restaurants in North Fulton offer the small-town atmosphere and gourmet cuisine that have made the Roswell Mill so popular. Roswell's original post office and general store, built adjacent to the public square in 1839, was an appealing location to Steve Nygren, owner of the Peasant Group. He acquired the facility in 1976 and fully restored the original flooring, brickwork and ceiling beams, creating a cozy historic setting for fine dining in North Fulton at the Public House.

# Robert Farley

With a golden track record which has included establishing the internationally acclaimed Alaska Repertory Theatre and directing the Atlanta-based production of Driving Miss Daisy, artistic director Robert Farley has been a welcome newcomer to the North Fulton arts scene.

His brainchild, the Georgia Ensemble Theatre, is a company-based nonprofit theatrical outfit based at the Roswell Municipal Auditorium, which has brought unique educational opportunities in the performing arts and top quality productions to the North Fulton stage.

"The cultural community in this area is unifying and creating a cultural identity for North Fulton," says Farley. "As an artist I love starting and building theaters. I'm dedicated to the design of the resident ensemble where artists work as a cohesive unit to master their craft."

The Georgia Ensemble Theatre, which was established in 1991, is patterned after the American Conservatory Theatre in San Francisco, where Farley worked as a free-lance stage director early in his career. He is also recognized for his work with the APA/Phoenix Repertory Company on Broadway, Huntington Hartford in Hollywood and the Coconut Grove Playhouse in Miami.

As artistic director of the Alliance Theatre in Atlanta, Farley generated the highest attendance and revenue in the theater's history, and the highest subscription rate in the country. In addition to the two-year sell-out performance of Driving Miss Daisy in the United States, Farley staged productions in Moscow, Leningrad and Shanghai, China.

His most recent venture brings a new level of artistic expertise to North Fulton.

"The resident ensemble design builds a rapport between the artists and the community they are serving," says Farley. "The goal is to infect the people with the enthusiasm to come to the theater regularly by having the actors on the streets and in the fabric of the community."

A core group of actors and actresses train through the theater's Conservatory, an in-house drama school which also offers upper-level classes to the community. During the season, guest artists are invited to join the central cast in the series of productions, which includes musicals, romantic comedies and light dramas.

Another popular historic spot is Lickskillet Farm House on Old Roswell Road at Rockbridge. The fully restored 1842 farmhouse creates a homey atmosphere of Southern hospitality featuring an excellent blend of American and Continental cuisine. The setting with its trout stream and nearby rustic gazebo is a popular location for private parties and receptions.

For real history buffs, Gene & Gabe's Lodge on Canton Street in upper Roswell Square is the place to dine. The Roswell Masonic Lodge held meetings in the upper floor of the building which they purchased from the builder Charles Dunwoody in 1868. Guests can dine al fresco on the second-floor porch, overlooking the charming town square, at the restaurant which has been at that location since 1977.

In addition to fine dining, the Roswell Mill has served in the past as a showcase for work by local and regional artists. Building C of the mill complex, a 10,000-square-foot multi-level artist's studio and gallery, was originally established as an artists' cooperative, and also functioned for a brief period as a fine art gallery under the direction of curator Joseph Perrin.

Perrin, a familiar figure in Atlanta art circles, is the retired chairman of the Department of Art at Georgia State University, where he served for 29 years. He is also the chairman of the M.A.R.T.A. Arts Council and of the High Museum in Atlanta.

To establish the gallery and attract a leading curator like Joseph Perrin, the Roswell Mill management team worked closely with the Roswell Arts Alliance.

In addition to community exhibits, the 135-member nonprofit organization sponsors demonstrations, classes, art workshops, films and presentations which are open to members and visitors to the Community Activity building in Roswell. The Alliance participates in annual shows at Bulloch Hall in December and February, the Roswell Fine Arts Festival on the town square and the Octoberfest celebration by area merchants.

The organization publishes a monthly newsletter listing the group's activities, particularly the guest

*Wedding, Roswell*

speakers and art-related events around the North Fulton community. Each spring they host a juried art competition for area high school students which is exhibited at the fine arts center in the Roswell Area Park on Woodstock Road, and present a scholarship to a North Fulton senior who is particularly gifted in an area of fine art.

As part of the recent efforts by Roswell's civic and business leaders to attract tourists to the historic district, the Roswell Arts Alliance has been asked to compile an art tour of the area with members of the organization acting as guides.

One stop on an art tour of Roswell and North Fulton would have to be the Roswell Visual Arts Center, which opened in the Roswell Area Park on Woodstock Road in October 1990. The state-of-the-art studio and gallery offers a wide variety of art classes and hands-on art experiences to local residents. The 4,100-square-foot center was designed for use as a visual arts center, with special attention placed on the lighting and gallery space.

The high school art competition "Art Attack" is jointly sponsored each spring by the Visual Arts Center and the Roswell Fine Arts Alliance. Young artists from the five North Fulton high schools display their work at the gallery in the park and compete for a $500 scholarship.

Other points of interest on an art tour of North Fulton would be the Ann Jackson Gallery on Canton Street. The family-owned business has been in operation in Roswell since the early 1960s, and features fine art, museum pieces and sculpture. Heaven Blue Rose, a contemporary gallery of fine art, is also on Canton Street. Although a newcomer to the North Fulton art scene, the gallery, which displays works in oil, water color, acrylic and mixed media, is a refreshing addition to the traditional galleries.

Other fine art establishments include Gallery V. Ltd., Artistic Glass, Nature by the Mill, The Dutch Palette and Mountain Star Studios. These unique centers offer everything from stained glass to original paintings and sculptures by teaching artists Greta Schelke, Teena Watson and Don Haugen.

The performing arts add an important dimension to the cultural experience of living in North Fulton. The Roswell Dance Theater, the area's oldest dance company, brings traditional and modern dance to audiences of schoolchildren and the general public in North Fulton.

The 65-member company was formed from the

*Wills Park Equestrian Center*

100

Tolbert-Yilmaz School of Dance in 1979 by founder Nancy Tolbert, a Roswell native and member of the Southern Ballet. Young dancers drawn from more than 1,000 students each season make up the talented ensamble, which performs at special events across the southeast like Atlanta's Festival of Trees and the annual North Carolina Dance Festival.

Community theater first came to North Fulton in 1990 in the shape of the dual-stage Village Center Playhouse, which sought to bring well-known productions by professional groups as well as original works by local artists to an eager North Fulton audience. The group specialized in lighthearted comedies and family classics which would appeal to audiences of all ages.

Artistic director Jared Shaver and partners Roy Rasband and Andy Miyakana created the theater from an abandoned movie house. The facility's primary stage, the Theater in the Round, appeals to family audiences with ongoing musicals, comedies and light entertainment, and averages seven shows a year including traditional family favorites like A Christmas Carol. A proscenium stage was created to offer an alternative for community groups in need of a place to perform. Productions on that stage include original dramas, mysteries and comic works.

The Georgia Ensemble Theatre, newcomer to the performing artist community in North Fulton, is a company-based, nonprofit theatrical outfit which will be bringing both unique educational opportunities in the performing arts and top-quality productions to the area. The project has been taking shape since the fall of 1991 and is the brainchild of artistic director Robert Farley, the nationally recognized director of the two-year sold-out production of *Driving Miss Daisy* at Atlanta's Alliance Theatre.

His most recent venture in North Fulton, patterned after the American Conservatory Theatre in San Francisco, will be based at the Roswell Municipal Auditorium. In the ensemble theater concept, a core group of a dozen actors and actresses work as a cohesive unit to master their craft and build a rapport with the audience they

*Roswell Square, July 4th*

are serving. Throughout the production season, guest artists are invited to join the central cast.

During the record-breaking three-play premiere season, the group played to more than 7,000 theatergoers and had a subscription audience of almost 2,000.

The ready support of this new project is evidence of the unifying cultural identity in North Fulton. Another sign is the formation of Fulton Arts North, an arts coalition created by the Fulton County Arts Council in 1992. The goal of the group is to stimulate support, facilitate communication and unify cultural organizations like the Georgia Ensemble Theatre, the Village Center Playhouse

and Orchestra Atlanta. The organization produces a semi-annual newsletter listing events of interest in the arts in North Fulton.

Dating from the era of visionary homebuilders like Howard Chatham to the key players in the 1990s residential market, elegant subdivisions with amenities like swimming pools and tennis courts have always been an affordable choice for North Fulton home buyers. Country club communities with magnificent homes built around perfectly manicured golf courses attract national sports figures, top-level executives and Atlanta families seeking a more relaxed, suburban life.

Transforming the rich farmland of North Fulton into golf courses is not a new concept to developers. As growth spread steadily north of the Atlanta perimeter, astute planners recognized the recreation potential in the rolling terrain and natural beauty of North Fulton, and have built more private golf courses there than in any other region of metro Atlanta.

The bulk of the courses have been built in two

distinct generations. Land developers, quick to identify a golf club as an amenity that facilitated home sales in the early 1970s, encouraged the population surge up the "Golden Corridor" of Georgia 400. A similar real-estate boom resulted in the construction of five luxury golf-course developments in Alpharetta in the mid-1980s.

The first wave began when, as the demand for golf increased, the courses were used as a drawing card to sell homes in the rural, undeveloped countryside of North Fulton. Investors, hoping to entice residents to move north from Atlanta, developed large tracts of land into communities with full countryclub amenities, including golf courses.

Brookfield West, in Roswell, which opened in 1972, was the leader in the first generation of private club communities that have become a hallmark of life in North Fulton. Developed by Chatham Land Development, the course cost over $1 million to build and has been host to both the Georgia State Open and the LPGA Lady Tara Classic in past years. The 165-acre course weaves around a community of stately executive homes that are still popular among homebuyers today.

When construction was completed on the course at Brookfield West, Chatham Land Development began work on a course on the other side of Georgia 400 at Willow Springs. The course and surrounding neighborhood were developed around a 27-acre lake, with full country-club amenities including pool, tennis courts and clubhouse. In 1985, the private club became member-owned when 350 club members purchased the facility from Arvida, the third owner of the property.

Three miles away, Rivermont Country Club on Nesbit Ferry Road was under construction in 1974. David Cupid, former golf professional at Ansley and Dunwoody country clubs, who bought the 800-acre property from Equitable, designed the home community around a golf course and country club.

In the late 1970s, contemporary homesites were finished around a 6,800-yard course designed by Disneyworld golf-course guru Joe Lee. An additional phase of cluster homes has been added to the remaining property at Rivermont in recent years, and like many North Fulton country-club communities, sales continue to be strong.

Joe Lee is also the design wizard behind the 18-hole course at Horseshoe Bend Country Club on Holcomb Bridge Road. Several holes on the rolling greens parallel the Chattahoochee River, which is in demand for homesites as well. In 1980, Horseshoe Bend became the national headquarters for the American Junior Golf Association and the host course for players ages 14–18 to compete in the annual Rolex Tournament of Champions.

Low-maintenance cluster homes with golf-course views are currently being developed at Horseshoe Bend, as well as estate properties with views of the Chattahoochee River. Home prices in the estates range from $400,000 to $1 million and heavily wooded property is available up to one acre.

The connection between upscale residential communities and golf course development gave rise to a second generation of private courses in the 1980s. Recent demographic research conducted by Club Marketing Corporation, a Texas-based firm, found North Fulton to be one of the most competi-

tive markets for golfing facilities in the South, and many of those courses were built during this second surge of construction.

First among the second wave of courses was the 850-acre luxury complex Country Club of the South, designed by renowned PGA champion Jack Nicklaus, located in Alpharetta. The community is home to some of Atlanta's favorite sports figures including many players for the National League Champion Atlanta Braves.

Sprawling homes priced from $300,000 up to several million dollars are built around the golf course on rolling hills adjoining Jones Bridge Park and the Chattahoochee River. In addition to use of the 40,000-square-foot clubhouse, pool, and ten

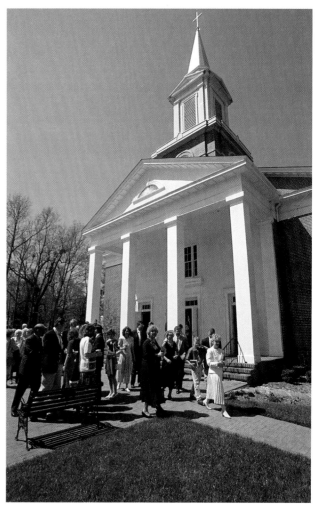

*First Baptist Church Roswell*

103

lighted tennis courts, residents can use any of the pool and playground facilities built throughout the community.

Country Club of the South attracts the golf industry's national spotlight to Atlanta each year as the host facility for the PGA Senior Tour Nationwide Championship. Eleven of the eighteen holes are played over water, but with five tees on every hole, the course can be enjoyed by amateurs as well as professionals.

Further north in Fulton County the rolling terrain and native hardwood trees provide an ideal environment for the Atlanta National Golf Club and the surrounding home community which opened in 1987. The development is set in the middle of the equestrian community off New Providence Road north of Crabapple Corners.

The zoysia fairways and lush greens of the Atlanta National course make for a challenging round of golf. The course has been ranked as one of the toughest facilities in the state by the Georgia State Golf Association.

A more "forgiving" course was designed by golf legend Tom Fazio and developed by North Fulton Land Equity at St. Ives in Alpharetta. The 600-acre golf-course community was host to the 1988 Street of Dreams, a national showcase of luxury homes. The European stacked-stone and traditional brick architecture of the homes, which are priced from $300,000 to $1.5 million, is enhanced by a full country-club amenities package including pool, tennis courts and clubhouse.

St. Ives is one of the few equity country clubs in the Atlanta market and a popular home community for families relocating to North Fulton. When United Parcel Service moved its national headquarters to Atlanta in 1992, St. Ives became one of the hottest-selling communities, attracting more than 44 families to purchase homes in the development because of the well-priced homes and high-quality amenities.

Several communities in the North Fulton area have been selected to host the prestigious Street of Dreams, including Thornhill, which features estate-style properties along the Chattahoochee River, and Nesbit Lakes, a more moderately-priced neighborhood of executive homes by Brooks-Horton Development.

Estate homes at Windward, the 3,400-acre, mixed-use community in Alpharetta, have also been featured in area home tours. The development combines a residential community of eight neighborhoods offering a variety of home styles priced from $140,000 to $800,000, and a 1,500-acre business park with space for office, retail and industrial development sites ranging from one to 100 acres.

The property was assembled by Mobil Land Development in the 1970s for use as a residential and commercial development built around a 195-acre man-made lake which provides fishing and water sports to the residents. The Windward Lake Club offers private tennis, swim and marina facilities, and a sports park with areas for picnicking, baseball, football, basketball and soccer.

*Gardener at the Janet Rothberg Home*

Many service and social organizations which support local agencies and charitable foundations have developed through interest by the residents of the community. The Windward Women's Club was formed in 1986, the Windward Association of Retired Men was formed in 1988, and since then, other community groups have banded together like the Windward Garden Club, Bridge Club and Bible-reading Club.

Twenty years after the property was initially assembled by Mobil, there are approximately 1,000 homeowners in Windward and 6,500 people employed in the Windward Business Park. The growing commercial development is already home to AT&T, Digital Communications Associates, Holiday Inn Worldwide, GE Capital, and UPS.

A most attractive feature of the Windward lifestyle is the newly completed Golf Club of Georgia which opened in 1991 off Windward Parkway. A private club owned and operated by Fuji Development Georgia Ltd., it was ranked number one by the U.S. Golf Association in a list of the top 25 toughest golf courses in Atlanta. It is a golfer's delight, offering 36 holes of championship play designed by Arthur Hills and a 53,000-square foot clubhouse.

The Lakeside and Creekside courses at the golf-only club are valued at more than $30 million each and have attracted a very selective market of international players to the North Fulton community. The Lakeside Course at Golf Club of Georgia was selected as the best new private course in the U.S. by *Golf Digest* in 1991, one of the highest honors in the golfing industry.

Arthur Hills also designed the new Standard Club off Abbotts Bridge Road in Alpharetta. The club, an Atlanta institution since 1867, moved to North Fulton in 1987 after negotiating a land settlement with Technology Park Atlanta.

Members of the Standard Club accepted 300 acres of the 2,000-acre John's Creek development in Alpharetta in exchange for their former location, a 165-acre site near Lenox Square mall in Atlanta. A 6,900-yard, par-72 course, designed to conform to the rustic setting of rolling hills and abundant pine trees, was completed in the late 1980s. A full-service clubhouse with indoor tennis facilities, banquet din-

*Christmas lights on private home*

ing capabilities, swimming pools and exercise areas was also built at the North Fulton location.

The Atlanta Athletic Club made a similar move to the suburbs two decades earlier. Home to golf legend Bobby Jones, the club was chartered in 1898 as a downtown athletic facility. As growth spread north of Atlanta, the membership was irreparably divided by the development of a 618-acre "River Bend" site on Medlock Bridge Road in 1967. Those choosing to remain in town eventually purchased the original East Lake facility, forming a separate club.

The initial 27-hole course designed by Robert Trent Jones opened for play at the Northside location in 1967 and was later upgraded to 36 holes based on design specifications by George Fazio. Host to such prestigious tournaments as the U.S. Open, the PGA Championship, the Junior World Cup, the U.S. Mid-Amateur and most recently, the 1990 U.S. Women's Open, the Highlands and Riverside courses are a credit to the members who pioneered the new location.

The Atlanta Athletic Club has also been selected to host international competitions in other sports, including the 1993-95 AT&T Challenge, an international tennis championship and one of only nine stops on the worldwide ATP Tour.

World tennis champions Andre Agassi, Jimmy Connors and Michael Chang were among the roster of star players charging the net at the 1994 tournament, which featured 32-man singles and 16-team doubles fields competing for $300,000 in prize money.

The tournament, which draws thousands of spectators from all over the southeast, was held since 1985 at Horseshoe Bend Golf and Country Club, but relocated in 1993 to a specially constructed stadium court facility at the Atlanta Athletic Club. In addition to the world class tennis, ProServ Inc., the Atlanta-based management company coordinating the tournament, scheduled a variety of special events around the competition including a concert by

*Children's fishing derby*

Orchestra Atlanta, a golf pro-amateur tournament with local celebrities and a tennis Pro-Am clinic and round-robin competition.

Private clubs and residential communities are not the only alternative for the thousands of avid North Fulton golfers. According to the National Golf Federation, an estimated 450,000 golfers in Georgia play on 281 private, municipal or daily-fee courses each year. North Fulton is a haven for golf enthusiasts with more than a dozen private facilities and several daily-fee courses offering a challenging round throughout the year.

Golf-course construction began as early as the 1930s, to meet the growing demand for the sport in North Atlanta, at the North Fulton Golf Course at Chastain Park. Built during the Depression by the Work Projects Administration on West Wieuca Road in Chastain Park, it is one of Atlanta's busiest public courses, supporting more than 85,000 rounds per year.

Other daily-fee courses in North Fulton are

The Champions and RiverPines. The two award-winning Alpharetta courses help to meet the demand for quality public golf facilities for North Fulton residents.

The Champions, built on the scenic equestrian countryside near Hopewell Road, is a public course with a private-course atmosphere. The course, which opened in 1991, was designed by ABC golf analyst and commentator Steve Melnyk and golf-course architect D.J. DeVictor. The rolling hills and evergreen areas along the 6,725-yard course make The Champions a challenging but enjoyable course for players of every skill level.

Golf lessons, group clinics and private instruction are available through the Golf Academy of Georgia at The Champions. Beginners can learn basic golf skills in a mixed clinic or perfect their strokes in private lessons with the staff professionals.

Lessons and clinics are also a popular recreational pursuit for North Fulton natives at RiverPines, a full-service daily-fee golf course in Alpharetta. The facility was developed on family farmland on Old Alabama Road by former AT&T executive Roger Mier. A par-three short course was initially developed on the site, which borders the Chattahoochee River and the prestigious Country Club of the South, and a full 18-hole course, designed by Dennis Griffith & Associates, opened shortly afterwards. The once rolling farmland has lent itself beautifully to sprawling tree-lined fairways and gently undulating greens on the 6,511-yard, par-70 course, as well as a spacious driving range and putting green.

In addition to golf, North Fulton offers a host of other recreational pursuits. Private and county-operated facilities field competitive teams in athletic programs like tennis, swimming, soccer and baseball, to name just a few.

Most North Fulton neighborhoods with swim and tennis amenities, and all the private country clubs, sponsor several men's, women's or junior teams to compete in the multi-tiered structure of the Atlanta Lawn Tennis Association. Of the 71,000 members registered throughout the five-county metro-Atlanta area in 1992, 18 percent are North Fulton residents.

The ALTA organization, founded in 1971 by a

*Chattahoochee River rowing*

*Craftsman Mike Rothberg*

vidual participants pay a $12 membership fee to the ALTA organization each year.

During the spring and fall, women can participate in a Thursday morning ladies league of teams, or in the Sunday businesswomen's league, which was added in 1973. Citywide participation in both leagues is very high, with 1,044 Sunday league teams and 683 Thursday league teams in the 1993 spring season.

Although the tennis is highly competitive on many levels, ALTA's popularity has skyrocketed as a social activity for North Fulton residents. Friends form teams through individual neighborhoods and often the race for post-game refreshments is more strenuous than the competition on the courts.

Team competition is also popular in soccer in North Fulton, home to the Atlanta Datagraphic Lasers, a semi-professional team which was founded by George Baker in 1978. The group was originally called Atlanta Magic, but when the team joined the U.S. Interregional Soccer League, a 43-team competitive league formed in 1986, the name was changed to reflect the owner, Datagraphic Soccer Club. As enthusiasm for competitive soccer has gained momentum in the southeast, North Fulton fans have been turning up for practices or games at the team's soccer complex on Arnold Mill Road in Roswell.

Team competition is equally rigorous at Swim Atlanta in Roswell, one of the area's most popular aquatic centers. The North Fulton facility is one of three Atlanta locations which collectively field the area's largest competitive team of 450 swimmers ranging from young summer league members to national champions.

The facility was started by Jim Fraser and Chris Davis, two Auburn University swim team coaches, in 1977. The Roswell location was immediately popular, with more than 600 students participating in the swim school from the very first season.

Certified instructors at Swim Atlanta teach more than 1,800 people a year in addition to coaching the resident team. Though competition is primarily against other members of the southeastern region, Swim Atlanta has gained national recognition in recent years by winning the Georgia state

group of local volunteers, has grown steadily from the initial 1,000 members to become the largest local tennis organization in the country. Play is divided into 18 levels of AA, A, B and C men's and women's doubles teams which compete in the spring and fall, and mixed-doubles teams which compete in the summer and winter.

Matches for all groups consist of dual meets of doubles matches. Team schedules are determined by computer each season, and winning groups from each division compete for the city title against other teams from the five-county metro area. Winners in each division receive the highly coveted "bag tags," a symbol of success to area tennis enthusiasts. Indi-

championships and the junior nationals.

Many North Fulton residents participate in year-round instruction at Swim Atlanta, where classes for infants through adults run the gamut from basic swimming skills to pre-competitive perfection of specific strokes. A four-foot-deep training pool, used primarily for beginners, is kept bathwater warm to encourage calm confidence while mastering fundamental swimming techniques.

While North Fulton residents enjoy top-notch athletic competition in their own backyard, they also have easy access to the professional sports scene in Atlanta as well as collegiate level competition at nearby universities.

Many Atlanta-based recreational events, like the annual Peachtree Road Race, draw thousands of North Fulton residents as both spectators and participants. The July 4th race is sponsored by the Atlanta Track Club and draws more than 40,000 participants each year. The 10K run begins at Lenox Square mall in Buckhead and weaves through the tree-lined streets of Atlanta to the finish line in Piedmont Park.

North Fulton residents also benefit from the city of Atlanta's recent rise to prominence as an international player in the world sports arena. In addition to being home to the national championship baseball team the Atlanta Braves, the city attracted international attention by being selected as the host of the 1996 Summer Olympic Games.

The Georgia Dome, future site of much of the upcoming Olympic competition, is home base for the Atlanta Falcons and the host facility for Superbowl XXVIII in 1994. The luxurious, enclosed stadium, which also hosts the annual collegiate level Peach Bowl, has added a new dimension to sports for local football fans. For regular college games, football enthusiasts can cheer on the famous Georgia Tech Yellow Jackets or enjoy Georgia Bulldog competition "between the hedges" in Athens.

Fans of college and professional basketball have two top-level local teams to choose from, the Georgia Tech Yellow Jackets and the Atlanta Hawks. The Atlanta Knights, local members of the International Hockey League, have brought professional hockey back to Atlanta and even the professional auto racing circuit is accessible, at both Road

*Mother and children*

*Chamber Orchestra, Sandy Springs*

Atlanta and the Atlanta Motor Speedway.

Whether it's rappelling, canoeing, horseback riding or baseball, recreation in North Fulton County is characterized by state-of-the-art parks and recreation centers, well-trained staff and creative programming for both children and adults.

With more than 1,200 acres of land devoted to recreational amenities, the Fulton County Parks and Recreation Department has kept pace with the needs of the growing population since its formation in 1972.

The parks department was originally developed as a division of public works in Fulton County in the late 1960s to facilitate lighting at county ball fields. Since then the county-based operation has grown to include an active Clean & Beautiful Committee, a Design and Development division, and separate sections for parks, recreation and administration.

Currently there are 14 parks in North Fulton County, many with historic significance or designed for specific recreational pursuits. Unique facilities like the Abernathy Arts and Crafts Center, the Chattahoochee Nature Center, the Wills Park Equestrian Center and the North Fulton Tennis Center, provide a vast array of opportunities for rest and relaxation to area residents.

The North Fulton Tennis Center on Abernathy Road in Sandy Springs has been cited as one of the top 50 public tennis facilities in the country by *Tennis* magazine. The clubhouse and 24 tennis courts are enjoyed daily by local residents. All courts are lighted for night play and there is also a 1,000-meter jogging track circling the center.

The center consistently fields the second-highest number of teams in the Atlanta Lawn Tennis Association, a citywide competitive league which began in the 1970s. Collectively the North Fulton Tennis Center registers an average of 200 men's, women's and junior teams each season.

Recent improvements in the parks system include the development of recreation space at the 34-acre Ocee Park on Kimball Bridge Road in Alpharetta. This area is second only to Sandy Springs in its need for additional park space to meet the minimum national acreage standards, based on the 1990 population estimates and the Fulton Parks

*North Fulton softball*

master plan. According to the plan, proposed in April, 1990, Sandy Springs will need an additional 420 acres of park space by 2010 to meet the minimum standard of 5 acres per 1,000 residents.

The Hammond Park Community Center in Sandy Springs is providing recreational services for North Fulton children with special needs. Each year children who are mildly to moderately mentally handicapped, autistic, have learning disabilities, behavior disorders or are perceived to be "at risk" are able to attend a Special Recreation Services Center summer camp program sponsored by the Fulton County Parks and Recreation's Therapeutic Department.

The camp is an extension of the year-round program which works with students from Spalding, Woodland and High Point elementary schools as well as Sandy Springs and Ridgeview middle schools. Park staff members lead the children on 25 different hikes through county parks and organize recreational activities like rafting on the Chattahoochee or swimming at Lake Lanier.

The Hammond Park Community Center is also used for ongoing meetings by various community groups including the Sandy Springs Porcelain Artists, the Georgia Caged Bird Society, the Tri-Chem Painters and the Parakeet Club. The Sandy Springs Seniors meet regularly at the community center for bridge competition and monthly outings.

Ongoing classes in gymnastics, volleyball, tennis, aerobics and basketball are offered at the Hammond Park Gymnasium, a full-service indoor and outdoor recreation complex operated by Fulton County. Several levels of team tennis competition are also available through the Atlanta Lawn Tennis Association and the U.S. Tennis Association. Hammond Park is also the site of the county's annual Ping-Pong Tournament each summer.

Other creative solutions have been found to the parks crisis in Sandy Springs, through a land swap with Georgia Power to acquire Morgan Falls and the acquisition of the Big Trees area near the North Fulton Annex on Roswell Road. The playground in the park at Morgan Falls has been modified for the physically disabled, a project of the Sandy Springs Optimists, who also revamped the facilities at Hammond Park in Sandy Springs.

At Big Trees, county officials are working with a citizens group led by John Ripley Forbes, a local naturalist active in the establishment of the Chattahoochee Nature Center, to develop the ten acres as a nature preserve.

The 200-year-old hardwood trees, rare native orchids and wildlife are in the middle of an area of intense development along Roswell Road, adjacent to the North Fulton Annex. The land was purchased in 1991 for $3 million with a combination of public and private funds. Grove Development, original owner of the property, donated three acres of flood plain to complete the 10-acre nature preserve.

Aggressive acquisition of potential park space like Big Trees strengthens community involvement in the Fulton County Parks program, a critical goal of the county's master plan which charts growth and development of the department through the beginning of the next century.

The community also plays a visible role in the maintenance and ongoing refurbishment of the Chattahoochee River Park, a 772-acre stretch of Azalea Drive along the banks of the Chattahoochee River. The winding stretch of river bank is the ideal place for family recreational pursuits like boating, fishing and picnicking. Although the majority of

*Chattahoochee River rowing races*

the land has been preserved as marshland, the park has picnic equipment, an extensive playground, boat launch and nature trail.

Rafting on the Chattahoochee is a time-honored Atlanta tradition, and kayaks, rafts and rowboats are a familiar sight at the river park, the last take-out point before Morgan Falls Dam. Visitors can also access the river at Morgan Falls and enjoy the two-mile float to Johnson Ferry. Watercraft can be rented from the Chattahoochee Outdoor Center between early May and Labor Day at Johnson Ferry and Powers Island.

Additional recreational sites along the Chattahoochee corridor include picnic facilities and hiking trails at Island Ford and Vickery Creek, as well as a boat launch at Jones Bridge Park. Collectively the three state parks offer approximately 600 acres of park space to North Fulton residents.

The Chattahoochee River Park is home to the Atlanta Rowing Club, the host organization for the regional collegiate rowing competition established in North Fulton in 1973.

The club has put the city on the map in rowing circles by sponsoring the "Head of the Chattahoochee," the third largest regatta in the country, each fall. In the last decade the annual river race held at the River Park has become as popular as traditional rowing competitions in other major cities like Philadelphia and Boston.

During the "Head of the Hooch," the rowing club has 1,500 athletes competing and draws more than 3,500 spectators. The rowers race against the clock 3.5 miles up the Chattahoochee River from Morgan Falls to the River Park on Azalea Drive. In the past, athletes representing as many as 78 schools and clubs have participated.

Record numbers of Atlanta rowing fans turn out to picnic, cheer on local favorites and celebrate this time-honored competition along the banks of the river. On race day, VIPs view the competition from a steward's enclosure, patterned after the elegant setting of the crew races in Henley, England.

The Atlanta Rowing Club's junior program, comprised initially of Milton High School students, prepares children ages 13–18 for competition against other clubs in the southeastern region. The club also

*11-year-old boys' soccer*

functions as host for area college teams including Georgia State, Georgia Tech, Emory and the University of Georgia.

New members are attracted to the club by the three-week clinics held monthly each spring, where trained instructors introduce the rudiments of the sport to small groups and encourage immediate participation. The novice clinics are limited to twelve people but are open to all ages. Levels of competition are determined by the rower's age and level of experience.

All rowing club members are welcome to use any of the club's 40 boats and have access to the 27,000-square-foot boathouse which was completed in 1989. The $170,000 facility on Azalea Drive is opposite the launch site in the River Park and is primarily used for boat storage. Future plans for the facility include the addition of locker rooms on the second floor.

113

*PGA Senior Tour, Country Club of the South*

In past years, the Atlanta Rowing Club has won the national championship and competed in the world rowing championship in the "Masters Category," for adults age 27 and up. Representatives of that group also compete in the rowing division of the Georgia State Games.

In addition to rafting and rowing, the Chattahoochee River National Recreation Area is a popular spot for hiking and stream fishing in North Fulton. The Vickery Creek Trail, one of only three trails in north Atlanta, is open to hikers as well as people using all-terrain bikes. The recreational area is a popular training ground for members of the Southern Off-Road Bicycling Association, a group of approximately 200 mountain-bike enthusiasts based

in Atlanta. The organization, formed in 1989, regularly tours Vickery Creek.

Fly fisherman in waders are also a familiar sight along the Chattahoochee River banks, where anglers enjoy catching the abundant trout, bream and catfish that are native to the stream. A valid Georgia fishing license is required for anyone 16 years of age or older and live bait fish may not be used. The Chattahoochee River downstream from Buford Dam to Roswell Road is open to trout fishing, which requires an additional license.

Fishing enthusiasts also enjoy the many lakes close to North Fulton including Allatoona, Lanier, Hartwell, Jackson, Sinclair, Oconee and Seminole which have open seasons for bass, trout and freshwater fishing.

The Geosphere Environmental Education Training Center in Alpharetta is also part of the Chattahoochee River National Recreation Area. A rustic, four-bedroom home called "The Lodge" on Barnwell Road serves as the focal point of the center, which offers ongoing environmental camps and programs for North Fulton students and teachers.

The center is partnered with the Georgia PTA, the U.S. Environmental Protection Agency, the Audubon Society and the Georgia Department of Natural Resources. Programming at the facility began in 1990 and is orchestrated by a group of volunteers.

A few miles down the Chattahoochee River, hidden behind the hustle and bustle of traffic on Roswell Road and Georgia 400, another natural oasis is tucked into the Roswell hillside.

The Chattahoochee Nature Center, an environmental education facility operated by Fulton County Parks and Recreation, is home to opossums, snakes, owls, kingfishers and a wealth of wildlife. The center occupies more than 100 acres of river marsh, freshwater ponds and wooded uplands on the banks of the Chattahoochee River on Willeo Road. It is an active community educational resource providing well-maintained exhibits and educational programming suitable for all ages.

Developed in 1976 through private-sector pressure on Fulton County, the Georgia Historic Trust Fund and the Natural Science for Youth Foundation, the nonprofit center is the ideal training ground and family entertainment facility for local naturalists.

Over the years, family programs like the Halloween Hikes, summer 'Possum Trot', and annual Painted Rock festival, have drawn crowds of North Fulton residents. More than 200,000 people visit the center each year to learn about natural science or just visit with the birds and fish along the marsh boardwalk.

A 27-acre parcel of land adjacent to the center was donated by the Joseph B. Whitehead Foundation and will soon be incorporated as additional office space and an educational center focusing on the importance of the Chattahoochee River. A portion of the new property is coniferous forest, which will complement the existing marsh trail and deciduous forest trail, providing three distinct environments for exploration.

A second nature preserve is being developed in Alpharetta, at Autry Mill, a 30-acre tract owned by the Atlanta-Fulton County Water Resources Commission. Fulton County is currently negotiating the purchase or long-term lease of the historic site. Identified as an ecologically significant area in a study by naturalist Dr. Charles Wharton in 1972, Autry Mill

was designated as a future nature preserve by the county in the comprehensive plan adopted in 1978.

Although funding is very limited, residents of the surrounding Ocee community are committed to the preservation of the property which consists of a partially restored, five-room fieldstone farmhouse, an early-20th-century barn and dilapidated chapel. According to a history compiled by Fulton County, after a variety of owners, the home, guest house and chapel were renovated by the deBray family in the 1970s.

Both the rare trees and foliage on the 280 acres surrounding the original 19th-century corn and wheat mill, and the buildings themselves, are historically significant and worthy of preservation. The ruins of the mill and dam are located below the farmhouse along Sal's Creek. Volunteers currently conduct tours of the nature preserve and provide special programming.

Providence Outdoor Recreation Center in Alpharetta offers another unique environment for North Fulton residents to experience the wonders of nature firsthand. The center is set in a 42-acre pine and hardwood forest with a 28-acre lake, surrounding wetlands and a natural rock quarry.

*Roswell Mill concert*

*Hobbyist at Roswell Air Force Base*

Resident naturalists conduct classes in rappelling, basic rock climbing, kayaking and camping survival skills. Outdoor adventure camps and specialty camps are also held at the sprawling complex on Providence Park Drive. Periodic canoe trips to southeastern waterways like the Nantahala River are also sponsored by the recreation department staff.

Providence is the meeting place for the North Fulton Bass Club, the Appaloosa Horse Club and the North Fulton Community Band. The rustic outdoor setting of the recreation center is also ideal for use by area scouting troops.

The hub of equestrian activities in North Fulton is Wills Park, a full-scale recreation facility operated by Fulton County in Alpharetta. Equestrian enthusiasts from all over the southeast gather at the 46-acre complex throughout the year for the finest horse shows, jumping competitions and rodeos in the state.

Prompted by members of the North Fulton Saddle Club, Fulton County built an open show ring and 150 stalls on the 50 acres of Wills Park in 1970.

The facility opened with only 14 shows, but as development continued to race north and horsing enthusiasts settled in the rural areas of Roswell, Crabapple and Alpharetta, the number of annual events has grown to over 100.

In 1987, Alpharetta was named the horse capital of the South by *Thoroughbred South* magazine. At that time, the economic impact of raising and training horses— specifically the quarter horses, thoroughbreds and Arabians which dominate the North Fulton equestrian industry— had developed into an enterprise producing $30-$50 million per year.

According to the Georgia Department of Agriculture, the horse industry contributes more than $200 million to the state economy annually. In North Fulton, the large number of training facilities and stables are responsible for a significant portion of this amount. Atlanta has the state's largest horse population and quarter horses are the most popular breed, according to the United States Equine Marketing Association.

Support for the sport increased and improvements

to the Wills Park facility were made, including two open arenas, a covered show ring with a glass-front announcer's booth and 298 permanent stalls. Thirty to fifty classes of horses, from Arabians to Palominos, are shown each year and competitions vary from traditional thoroughbred riding and jumping skills to rodeo acts like bareback bronco riding and steer wrestling.

More than 80 percent of the shows at the Alpharetta facility benefit local and national charities. One of the most popular events is the Georgia Hunter-Jumper Show, a two-week English-style riding and jumping competition which attracts more than 30,000 visitors and supports Scottish Rite Children's Hospital. Equally successful is the Southeastern Charity Horse Show, held each fall to benefit the Shepherd Spinal Center in Atlanta. The annual competition features 80 classes of saddlebreds and more than 450 horses.

The "granddaddy" event for the horsy set is the Atlanta Steeplechase. The afternoon of thoroughbred racing each April is the way North Fulton, indeed all of Atlanta, ushers in spring.

Riders compete for a purse of more than $180,000, one of the largest Steeplechase purses in the country. Proceeds from the race, which began in 1965, benefit the Atlanta Speech School.

The rural roots of North Fulton, which add a desirable charm and elegance to events like the Steeplechase, are evident in local programs like the Tailgate Farmers Market held weekly at Wills Park. Buyers and sellers of fresh homegrown produce gather every Saturday morning throughout the summer to hawk their goods from the back of pickup trucks, a scene reminiscent of the area's earliest merchants. The farmers are welcomed by Alpharetta residents and visitors from neighboring communities who come out in droves to snap up the freshest "Georgia-grown" goodies.

In the neighboring city of Roswell, the Recreation Department serves approximately 3,000 people daily and records more than 1 million registered participant visits annually in a wide variety of programs and community services.

Facility and program management is handled by the city's Recreation Department, which was

established in 1951 and has been named the Public Agency of the Year by the Georgia Department of Parks and Recreation four times. The organization was founded by a group of concerned citizens as the Roswell Recreational Committee. Their first fund-raiser, Roswell Youth Day, financed construction of municipal tennis courts near the old courthouse and eventually a baseball diamond for city use. The event has become a Roswell tradition and has been held the second Saturday in October since the early 1950s.

Activities are divided between the three main facilities maintained by the city, specifically the Roswell Area Park on Woodstock Road, Waller Park and the East Roswell Park.

The 80-acre Roswell Area Park is divided into 63 active acres featuring seven baseball/softball fields, twelve lighted tennis courts, a lighted walking/jogging trail, soccer field, football field, 50-meter outdoor swimming pool, family picnic shelters, two playgrounds and three major indoor recreation centers: the Community Activity building,

*Roswell Village Playhouse*

*Chastain Park concert*

the Physical Activity Center and the Visual Arts Center.

A variety of classes and athletic competitions are held in the Community Activity building, which contains classrooms, meeting space and two gymnasiums. In addition to the basketball court, one gymnasium has a mezzanine track and the other has a fully operational stage.

Roswell gymnasts train in the 23,500-square-foot Physical Activity Center. In addition to a large gymnastics room, the state-of-the-art facility has a training pit, auxiliary gym, bleacher area, two classrooms and administrative office space. The Roswell Gymnos, the city's competitive team, have been involved in gymnastic meets on both the state and national level.

The Visual Arts Center functions as both instructional space and as a gallery for local artists. Roswell residents can take classes in the arts or instruction in the studio, kiln room or photography darkroom.

As growth increased east of Georgia 400 in Roswell, the East Roswell Park and 26,000-square-foot community activity center on Fouts Road were developed in 1990. In addition to the indoor recreation center, the 38 acres of parkland include four baseball/softball fields, two soccer fields, a playground and picnic shelter and a walking/jogging trail. The recreation center has two gymnasiums, a game room and kitchen as well as art, dance and aerobics classrooms.

Waller Park Recreation Center and the Waller Park Extension are located at Oxbo and Dobbs Road between the north and south historic squares in the heart of Roswell. The facilities include a gymnasium, game room, three baseball/softball fields, a soccer field, two outdoor racquetball courts, two tennis courts and a playground.

In each center a variety of programs, classes, clubs and recreational instruction are available. City programs are often challenged by overwhelming participation figures, like youth baseball, which had as many as 1,400 children playing on 108

teams in the spring of 1993 during the height of the Atlanta Braves "fever." Each summer, record numbers also participate in the programs for children including aquatic lessons, visual art classes, day camps, performing arts, basketball, t-ball and gymnastics.

The Roswell Recreation and Parks Department sponsors several major events each year including an Easter Egg Hunt, Roswell Day with the Braves, the Roswell Arts Festival, a Field Day for the Developmentally Disabled and a Halloween Party.

Participation in children's programs is also high at the North Metro YMCA. In 1992, more than 2,500 children participated in baseball, soccer and basketball programs, 390 children were involved in the after-school program and 220 children attended summer day-camp.

While funds are being raised to build a permanent facility, programs organized by the YMCA are held at other locations around North Fulton. The goal of the campaign, "New Visions, Old Values," is to complete construction of a multi-purpose YMCA recreation complex by 2001.

Since May 1989, the North Metro YMCA has been headquartered on a 32-acre tract of donated land in Preston Ridge, a commercial and residential development off State Bridge Road in Alpharetta. The land, which will eventually house the full-service facility, was donated by the Perot Group, developers of the property. The site is currently used for the summer day-camp programs and a temporary petting zoo.

In the immediate future, the staff at the YMCA hope to add tennis and street hockey to the youth program. Additional recreational programs for children and adults will come on-line as dictated by the supply of equipment and adequate facilities. As residential growth continues to impact the need for quality recreational programs in North Fulton, groups like the North Metro YMCA seek to satisfy the needs of local residents with new facilities and expanded programming.

## ACKNOWLEDGMENTS

Each of the following corporate profile companies made a valuable contribution to this project. Longstreet Press gratefully acknowledges their participation.

Ahlstrom Recovery Inc.
City of Alpharetta
AT&T
Concourse
First Colony Bank
Fulton County Economic
   Development Division
Historic Roswell Convention
   & Visitors Bureau
Kimberly-Clark Corporation
Laing Properties/Huntcliff Summit
Drs. McDonald & Johnson Family
   Dentistry
North Fulton Regional Hospital
Northside Hospital
Reinhardt College, The North Fulton
   Center
J. Andy Keith and Misty M. Reid
   RE/MAX Affiliates North
City of Roswell
Roswell House Antiques & Gallery
Roswell United Methodist Church
Saint Joseph's Hospital of Atlanta
Scottish Rite Children's Medical Center
Windward– A Mobil Land Community


The following publications and organizations provided excellent sources for the text:

Garrett, Franklin M. *Atlanta and
   Environs*
DeVane, Ernest. *Roswell Historic Homes
   & Landmarks*
Walsh, Darlene. *Roswell– A Pictorial
   History*
Coogle, Lois. *Sandy Springs Past Tense*
Coogle, Lois. *More of Sandy Springs
   Past Tense*
*The Atlanta Business Chronicle*
*The Atlanta Journal Constitution*
*The Revue Newspaper Answer Book*
The Sandy Springs Historic Community
   Foundation
The Roswell Historical Society
North Fulton Community Charities
Data Book Inc.


We would also like to thank the following individuals who contributed in a variety of ways to the quality of *North Fulton: Toward the Twenty-First Century.*

Dottie Etris, Roswell Visitors Center
Zachary Henderson, Architect
Shayne Escher, North Fulton Senior
   Services
Jacque Coxe, The Teaching Museum
   North
James Watson, Fulton County Parks and
   Recreation
Nancy Tolbert-Yilmaz, Roswell Dance
   Theater
Mak Gebre-Hiwet, MARTA
Don White, Roswell City Councilman
Kevin Johns, Roswell City Planner
Emory Reeves, Crabapple
   Business Owner
Judy Webb, Ocee Community
Lee Sweeney, North Fulton Human
   Service Center
Sara Lunsford, Roswell Historical Society
Jerry King, Roswell Police Department
Dee West, Alpharetta Clean and
   Beautiful
Barbara Duffy

## PHOTO CAPTIONS

vi.   Spring 1990, Roswell
viii.  Tulips in bloom
120.  Vickery Creek, Roswell


## INDEX